TRIUMPH RAZOREDGE

RENOWN, 1800 & 2000

JOHN BATH

AMBERLEY

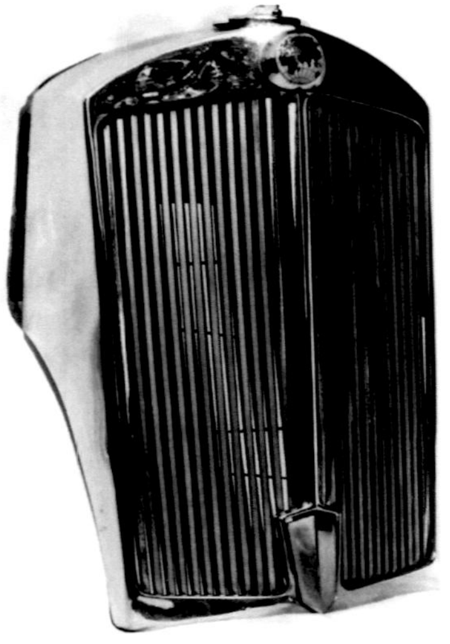

This book is dedicated to the memory of my late son, Andrew, with whom I enjoyed many hours at car rallies, museums and also riding in classic cars, though he did strongly favour American cars more than home-grown examples. Also to my wife, Sue, and daughters Caroline and Geraldine, who have put up with this pastime for so many years.

First published 2025

Amberley Publishing
The Hill, Stroud,
Gloucestershire, GL5 4EP

www.amberley-books.com

ISBN: 978 1 3981 2693 0 (print)
ISBN: 978 1 3981 2694 7 (ebook)

British Library Cataloguing in Publication Data.
A catalogue record for this book is available from the British Library.

Typeset in 10pt on 13pt Celeste.
Typesetting by SJmagic DESIGN SERVICES, India.
Printed in the UK.

Appointed GPSR EU Representative: Easy Access System Europe Oü, 16879218
Address: Mustamäe tee 50, 10621, Tallinn, Estonia
Contact Details: gpsr.requests@easproject.com, +358 40 500 3575

Contents

Acknowledgements

Where do you start with a project that has taken this long to come to fruition? I have met a great many people who have contributed directly or indirectly to this book over some fifty years. I will start with my TROC colleagues. Tom Robinson and I have almost worked in parallel to try to get to the bottom of the story of these cars, with Tom's knowledge of the Limousines being almost encyclopaedic. With former club Company Secretary Bob Parsons, both he and Tom were my introduction to the club that caters for these cars.

Roger Stone is the enthusiastic editor of the club newsletter, *The Globe*, and took over from Tom, who had 'only' edited the newsletter for some thirty-seven years!

Bernhard Ruest shares my enthusiasm for these cars, and we seem to like many other models as well beyond Standard-Triumph by a happy coincidence.

Mike Sampson has also contributed some superb photos of his Renown, while Bob Hobbs owns the gorgeous black LKV 541, which might have been in the company fleet when new with its original Coventry registration.

I am also very grateful to Nick Black, the youngest son of Sir John Black, for contributing the Foreword. I can think of no other person more appropriate, and therefore it was a huge relief when I received his agreement to do so.

I would like to thank the following people/organisations for permission to use copyright material in this book: TROC Ltd Archives, Bernhard Ruest, Herr Roscher of Roscher Classic Cars, Mike Sampson, Coventry Archives, Martin Care, David Wickens, David Siddom, BMIHT Gaydon for use of official Standard-Triumph factory photos, Nick Black for the portrait of Sir John Black and the late Harry Webster OBE.

From The Mayflower Club (TMC), I would like to thank James Chalk for his photo of the 'Mayflower' bonnet mascot, and I have shared many hours of research in the libraries of Gaydon and Coventry with Steve Coulman, the former Club Historian.

Phil Homer of the Standard Motor Club allowed me to quote from his extensive research into SMC production records, which revealed many new details.

For the Coventry Motor Museum, special thanks must be given to former employee Steve Bagley who allowed me to rifle through the Walter Belgrove Archives, and to Damien Kimberley, Archives & Local Studies Officer. While for BMIHT, Gaydon, I should like to thank Anders Ditlev Clausager, former Archivist, for statistical details and, more recently, Sarah-Jane Wilson of the Photographic Library.

Kyia Friesen, based in Oregon, saved Mayflower prototype X488 and Jason Dennis (now back in Scotland after a sojourn with his family in the USA) relayed the story of this remarkable survivor, currently owned by his uncle Dennis Delargy, both of whom are now based in Scotland.

From New Hampshire, USA, the recently deceased Richard Langworth told me the about the gestation of the landmark *Triumph Cars* history book, written jointly with the late Graham Robson.

Dave Pilcher from Texas allowed me to drive his rare Limousine in Texas, my first drive in such a car – one of the most courageous decisions he is likely to take!

Although I started the research when the newest Renown was only sixteen years old, I only really met key people who worked at the manufacturers or Mulliners of Birmingham in the 1980s when I often travelled to Coventry on business. That way I was able to have very pleasant chats with the late Harry Webster OBE at his home in Kenilworth, the late Vic Hammond, similarly at Pillerton Priors (also from Standard Motor Company), and the late Stuart Peck in Warwick from Mulliners. I owe a particular debt to these three gentlemen for the time I spent with them on many a winter's evening on a 'pit stop' when travelling back from a business meeting in Coventry or elsewhere in the West Midlands.

More recently I tracked down the late Alan Booth, who was based in Michigan in the university town of Ann Arbor, and he had been an SMC Apprentice when the Walter Belgrove-designed TRX (or 'bullet car') was brand new. He recounted seeing at least one of the only three of these cars made, of which two still survive; one was reported to in Germany at the time of writing.

Others who have played a part in this story are no longer with us but still deserve a thank you from me: Derek Cooper, who took some of the only colour photos of the first TROC Rally in 1976; David Blackwell of the Standard Motor Club, who allowed me to borrow copies of the production records; Peter Faber from Whangarei, New Zealand, with whom we stayed in 2007 and also researched local examples of the marque; Lothar and Karl-Heinz Klementz from Germany were both loyal club supporters for many years, providing invaluable local information; and the late Chris Hewitt, who was the longest-serving Chairman of the Triumph Razoredge Owners Club, with whom I spent many a happy hour or two in a local pub near Guildford, Surrey.

Uncredited images are the copyright of the author. My apologies go out to any of the many people I have met while preparing this book who have been inadvertently omitted despite their contribution.

My thanks also go to my wife, Jeremy Satherley and Tom Robinson for proofreading, though any mistakes must be laid at my door.

Finally, I must thank my commissioning editor, Alexander Stilwell, who approached me to write this book, and Alison Flowers, who saw me through the project.

Author's Note

Every attempt has been made to seek permission for copyright material used in this book. However, if we have inadvertently used copyright material without permission/acknowledgement we apologise and will make the necessary correction at the first opportunity.

Foreword by Nick Black

After the acquisition of Triumph in 1945, my father set about creating a new brand for the post-war period. His retrospective view of the 1930s era was largely influenced by the SS Jaguar range, including the limousine style produced by Mulliners of Birmingham in some of their custom-built bodies manufactured before the war, one of which John Black owned himself.

The Standard Motor Company had provided SS Cars with chassis and engines over an extended period, so had sufficient experience in developing plans for their future razor-edge styling.

Synonymous with their venture into new motor designs, Standard also embarked on large-scale tractor production after Sir John's celebrated meeting with Harry Ferguson in the August of 1945. Subsequently, the first vehicle coming out of the factory would be the Triumph Roadster, offered in 1800, and then 2000 versions in 1949.

But the TDB series of cars with their 108-inch and 111-inch chassis soon arrived, marked by that ubiquitous name Renown. These were produced between 1949 and 1954. Although the trouble it must have taken to extend the chassis by 3 inches now seems excessive, by allowing for a glass partition between chauffeur and passengers my father's passion for motoring in style and comfort was typified. Also, by utilising fold-down picnic tables attached to the lower part of this partition, it guaranteed a more civilised approach to motoring. Those intricate details certainly demonstrated John Black's propensity for comfort and elegance.

There is a wonderful story about him visiting Ivor Penrice, Standard's Publicity Manager, one evening with his chauffeur Frank Golding at the wheel. After drawing up to the house in Kenilworth, Frank alighted from his seat and walked around the back of the Renown to open the rear door on the other side for Sir John to step out. At the end of the occasion, with the whole process repeated and considering the vehicle was a good 15 feet long, Ivor remarked: 'Golding was certainly getting his exercise.'

So, the Triumph Renown stands today as a nostalgic emblem of a bygone era which my father firmly relished. Perhaps it was his partiality for neat lines and elegant styling which led him to co-operate with Walter Belgrove's drawings back in the early days of the Renown's inception. The legendary title 'razor-edge' well encompasses the whole concept of this prestigious automobile.

Nick Black and Bob Hobbs (for many years, TROC's Spares Officer) after a ride in Bob's immaculate Renown, Coventry-registered LKV 541.

From my own experience being brought up at Warninglid Grange in Sussex, I remember the six stables that all housed one of Daddy's cars to be treated with the utmost respect. Perhaps it was the 1954 Mk VI Bentley that held pride of place, but certainly the Renown would have been a close second, having served him initially for years, closely followed by the TR2, Mayflower, Standard Vanguard and finally the Humber Hawk Shooting Brake.

I met John Bath about ten years ago when he was visiting us in Stamford with a colleague's Renown, indeed a memorable occasion. Since then, we have been in communication about developments in the interest of these classics, although most people rarely know their origins. Therefore, John's book must surely be the culmination of nearly a lifetime of keen aspirations. I wish him and the TROC all success in their future endeavours.

Introduction

Why does anyone have hankerings to buy a Triumph Renown, just one example of the various Razoredge saloons produced by Standard-Triumph soon after the Second World War?

The story of my relationship with these cars starts, probably like many other classic car enthusiasts, with schoolboy ownership of a Dinky model car. It was a blue Triumph 1800 Saloon which I thought at the time was a Renown, the only long-term model name (as opposed to a number) applied to this series of cars. Incidentally, these cars are often confused with the smaller Mayflower because of the very similar 'razor-edge'

All five main body colours of the Dinky Triumph 1800 Saloon – the wheels were various colours.

David Shulver's trade box of 1800 Saloons shows how they were delivered to retailers in the early post-war years (individual boxes were used later).

(or 'knife-edge', as it was also once called) styling, so I will also mention this model in brief later. I loved the styling of this model 'Renown', which seemed to look just as good at any angle and therefore it was always my 'company car' as MD of whatever Dinkies I chose for my 'carpet fleet' at the time.

However, by complete contrast, I also admired the most up-to-date 1950s American car designs of the time. The common link could only be my own liking of certain specific cars as varied as American Buicks and British Rovers, though I must add straightaway that I had no skills or ambition to be a car designer.

I was to find out much later that the very similar looking 1800 and 2000 predecessor models were not truly Renowns. Then, later still, that there was a longer-wheelbase variation, plus a Renown Limousine, making five variations in all apart from the Mayflower. No wonder the earlier cars are retrospectively, but incorrectly, described as 'Renowns'.

Starting grammar school in Westcliff-on-Sea near Southend, Essex, in 1958, my form master and English teacher was Ron Coats (note: no 'e') for much of my time there. For some reason he was nicknamed, rather cruelly, 'Crippen'. He ran a black Renown, which was sadly totalled by a student and replaced by an equally handsome Daimler Consort – both cars bodied by Mulliners of Birmingham.

I am very grateful to Mr Coats for his excellent teaching over the years, but how ironic that the lessons I did not especially enjoy at the time, like sentence construction, proved to be the most useful in my later career as a general commercial insurance broker, working largely in the City of London.

Purchasing My Own Renown

I guess that, in consequence, I was destined to buy a Renown at some stage. A glance one night at the small ads in the *Southend Evening Echo* back in 1970 featured a grey 1951 Renown offering 'maximum 100 mph motoring and 26 mpg', though presumably not at the same time. It was also described as 'recently resprayed and re-chromed' and was available in nearby Thorpe Bay for the price £120 o.n.o.

Seen at dusk, it looked superb with its gleaming chrome, but there were various defects I failed to spot until after the inevitable purchase, at a negotiated £106. It was an emotional purchase, of course, and so began a five-year relationship with Commission Number TDB 4545 (in Standard-Triumph speak, as opposed to the usual term 'Chassis Number') combined with registration number FRD 144.

This car was originally from Reading and was first owned by a director of the town's London Road motorcycle dealers, Phillips & Bloomfield Ltd. Predictably, perhaps, the nickname 'Freddie Gross' was soon applied by my family.

I probably did around 25,000 miles in the car, including a regular commute and one wedding, where I was best man to my friends Lance and Ann, but I sold it in 1975 when I needed to concentrate all my funds into the purchase of a new house.

My 1951 Renown FRD 144 at our first house in Benfleet, Essex, 1973.

The buyer was my near namesake: John Bates, of whom more to come, who drove his new purchase back from Essex to the Wolverhampton area. I was now 'carless' and living at the top of a hill in our new Benfleet home.

A Tale of Two Renowns: MGP 100 and FRD 144

Long after I had sold FRD, I read a piece in a classic car magazine about the grandson of a former Renown owner featuring his grandfather's replacement car, a P6 Rover 2000TC, which was still in the family. I then followed a hunch with the co-operation of the magazine. That Renown's owner lived in Croydon, which was also the former base for MGP 100 when I snapped it in Essex in 1970 alongside my own car. It was very fortunate that my friend and former colleague Marc dropped the magazine on my desk at work one day, retrieving it from a plane after a business trip abroad; otherwise, I would have missed it.

By an amazing piece of good fortune, my hunch paid off. Soon, courtesy of the grandson and current P6 owner Martin Care, I was seeing his late grandfather's own photos of the Renown pairing, taken at the very same impromptu session in Eastwood, near Southend, Essex, plus others taken on holiday to Brighton, Snowdonia, etc., for the first time – almost fifty years later.

The late Sidney Pester's beautiful 1951 Renown MGP 100, seen in Brighton in its heyday in the early 1870s. (Courtesy of Martin Care)

A pair of 1951 Renowns in Essex in a chance encounter in a small close. MGP 100 and FRD 144, Eastwood, 1970.

I was reunited with FRD 144 in 2022 at Rothley (Great Central Railway) station, but it is now 461 UXA so I did not recognise it at first in its new paint job.

MGP 100 was easily the best original Renown I had seen in those far-off days. I should add here that I had recalled MGP 100 had been replaced by a P6 Rover, which did give credence to my detective work. Martin's grandfather, Sidney Horace Pester, had owned the Renown for some ten years, only selling it in early 1972. It was clearly his pride and joy, as was his subsequent P6, now handed down to Martin.

FRD 144 still survives at the time of writing in Derbyshire, though scarcely recognisable after having lost its cherished original registration number and its factory-applied Cotman (metallic) Grey colour in favour of black and white. However, we have since lost trace of MGP 100, also later re-registered and last seen in 'wedding white', as opposed to its gleaming black.

Triumph Razoredge Owners Club, est. 1975

By coincidence, the very year I sold my Renown – 1975 – was when the club devoted to the preservation of these cars was formed: the Triumph Razoredge Owners Club, or 'TROC' for short, later to become a limited company. John Bates, the new owner of FRD 144, was one of the founders of TROC and responsible for organising events.

The following year, 1976, the first National Rally was held at the Cotswold Wildlife Park & Gardens in Burford, Oxfordshire. The year 2025 will see TROC's fiftieth anniversary rally and a return to this very site, which happily is still in the hands of the same family.

The first TROC Rally at Cotswold Wildlife Park & Gardens, Burford, 1976. Bob and Liz Parsons' car is on the left.

Above and below: The first TROC Rally at Cotswold Wildlife Park & Gardens, Burford, by the late Derek Cooper, 1976.

Above: The late James Lea's beautiful 1951 Triumph Renown at his home. It still resides in Maine at the time of writing.

Right: A 1951 Triumph Renown on the 'wrong side of the road' in Rockport, Maine, USA – owned then by the late James Lea.

It is under the leadership of Reggie Heyworth, son of the late John Heyworth, the park's founder and our host at that time.

The original 1976 rally, held only twenty-two years after the last Renown was built, was hugely successful. Luckily for a fledgling event, examples of all five variations were present, with one example each of both the rare 2000 Saloon and the even less common Limousine.

Most of us present on the day had never seen a Limousine before. Some forty years later I was to drive this very car 'on the wrong side of the road' in Texas, USA. But that is another story.

TROC and My History of Renown Research

Once I had bought my Renown, I was to find that there was very little in print on the history of this model and its development anywhere, but gradually I started to build up a picture of the different variations for the first time. Indeed, over the years you could say that the less information could be easily found, the more determined I was to locate the background to the car's development and people involved in the project.

Along with the purchase, I was given a *Standard Vanguard Workshop Manual* (which also had sections covering the similarly mechanical-based Renown) plus a *Triumph 2000 Saloon & Roadster Handbook*, as well as the more relevant *Renown Handbook*.

I soon joined the Triumph Roadster Club (this was before TROC existed) and attended local meetings in Essex, with the object of comparing notes with other owners. This was how I encountered my very first Triumph 1800 Saloon – out in remote Maylandsea on the Dengie Peninsula, by the River Blackwater. Even though I was born and bred in the county, I had never heard of this Essex village.

After an earlier failed attempt to set up a Triumph 'Razor Edge Register' (RER for short), TROC was formed in 1975, which did prove to be a very long-term venture, though we probably could not see beyond the first couple of years at the time.

My first sighting of a Triumph 1800 Saloon in Maylandsea, Essex, 1971.

Those who had contacted RER had all been listed, fortunately, and those details compiled by the founder, Stanley Davies, were handed over to the then nascent TROC, though sadly Mr Davies seemed to disappear from view at this point.

Incidentally, from now on, I will only use the single-word version 'Razoredge' for the eponymous club and the relevant Triumph models, or 'razor-edge' for the style of cars more generally.

With my then new Renown purchase, joining the Triumph Roadster Club (TRC), which had been formed back in 1960, proved to be an excellent decision not long after purchasing my car. Because of my lack of knowledge, I got a lot of help from members such as Chris Manning, Paul Hawkins and John Seaman and found some parts of my home county never seen before.

Thanks to help from Chris, I even bought a second Renown RPC 70, which was beyond repair due to a corroded chassis. Inevitably, this was a black car – easily the most common colour. It was also another 1951 version, but this purchase was only bought to break for spares, notably later using its Overdrive gearbox in FRD 144.

Soon I felt confident enough to write an article on the five variations for the *Roadster Review*, then submitted it to the editor and it duly appeared in print.

However, saloon owners really needed a club they could call their own. Therefore, it was ironic that very soon *after* having sold my car, TROC had been formed.

The first TROC committee members I met were at St Pancras (my favourite London station) to pick up some NOS (new old stock) spares I had acquired but not fitted to my car. Little did I know then that these two complete strangers were to become lifelong friends. They were Tom Robinson from Sheffield and Bob Parsons from Uxbridge.

Soon I was passing on some spares that I had located after selling my car, including four brand-new large chrome 'nave plates', as Triumph preferred to call them, or hubcaps to most people. Then later, in 1975, I decided to join TROC.

Information relating to our cars was still sparse at that point and, as I was to find out later, not always accurate, even in factory publications, but at least I had previously made a start on writing about the differences between the various models. This was greatly helped by seeing and riding in that 1800 Saloon in Maylandsea, and I knew a little about the later 2000 Saloon from the handbook, as mentioned.

At this stage I had yet to see a 2000 Saloon, the equivalent of the second version of the Roadster, both models now modified to take Vanguard drivetrains. Incidentally, both 1800 and 2000 models had unusual right-hand column changes as new, though the first 1800 Saloon I had seen, mentioned earlier, had just been converted to floor change.

My Role Within TROC

I was later invited to be TROC's Honorary Historian, a good example of a 'kingdom of the blind' situation where I took on the role of the 'one-eyed man'. Subsequently, I also suggested renaming the club newsletter *The Globe*, the name that is still used today for the much-improved, full-colour club magazine.

Having researched these cars over some fifty years, it has astonished me how new information can still be revealed decades later – largely thanks to the help of TROC colleagues, members, complete strangers and former owners. A long period without any new finds would often be followed by a flurry of remarkable and unpublished information, perhaps from an unexpected new source. As many as possible of these indirect contributors – unsung heroes to me – are mentioned in the Acknowledgements and a great debt is owed to them all.

My role within TROC helped me significantly in locating new material, or information coming to me through *The Globe,* as compared with carrying out research in isolation in the early days of my Renown ownership. However, even now I feel I cannot call this book a 'complete story' to avoid being a hostage to fortune, having heard one writer put forward the notion that 'there was nothing else to be written about these models' back in 1991! Furthermore, I cannot put in all the detail I have, otherwise running the risk of the book becoming unreadable.

Incidentally, I must warn that the well-worn phrase about 'lies and statistics' most definitely applies to the officially published figures in Standard-Triumph literature. For instance, you would think the highest numbered Renown would be the last one made, but this is not so. We now know that the last Renown of all, a saloon model, went out the door with no fanfare, as was the norm at the time for a discontinued model. The Razoredge series of Triumphs just faded away at the end of October 1954 – the year after Mayflower production had ceased.

As will be seen, Standard Motor Company, or SMC for short, presumably confirmed to *Glass's Guide* (and probably other sources) that the highest numbered Renown, a Limousine, TDC 3000 LIM, was the last to be made. This was simply not correct; it was not even the last Limousine to be built, as will be revealed later.

I associate the colour black with Renowns because almost every example I saw, both on the road and in south-east Essex scrapyards of the 1970s when hunting for spares, was indeed painted thus. The two metallic shades, Cotman Grey and Jade Green, were much less common.

I only saw one Renown in maroon in those days, and no Comet Blue car ever came to light at that stage of my life, these usually being the only other choices available. However, in the final months of production you could seemingly order your new Renown in any colour you wanted, as the SMC production records were to reveal many years later. However, that last saloon was indeed painted black.

My research has taken place over fifty years. Over this time I have visited the Coventry Motor Museum and the British Motor Museum at Gaydon whose then archivist, Anders Ditlev Clausager (an award-winning author), must have spent many hours on the club's behalf going through the SMC production records, which covered both Standard and Triumph cars. This was a task that I was to carry out myself on a much smaller scale many years later, thanks to the generosity and trust of Standard Motor Club member (and one-time Flying Standard 20 V Eight owner) the late David Blackwell – once hailing from Thorpe Bay where I found my car.

David allowed me to borrow a large suitcase full of most of the 1954 SMC production records in about twenty thick files. I was to concentrate on just the final six months of Renown production in 1954, which is how I found out about the many unpublished options available during this period, mainly relating to paint and trim variations, including two-tone body colours.

Warwick University holds the board meeting minutes of Standard-Triumph, and initially I found these (most likely 'sanitised') versions of Triumph history to be disappointingly light on detail. Though years later, I can see that they did produce some examples of information not perhaps published before. For instance, an extract of the 1953 minutes revealed that Standard was in discussions with the owners of the American Jeep brand about producing their own version. They even had a brand name ready to apply to a putative new model or marque: Landguard. No doubt the success of the Land Rover as a companion make to Rover cars gave Sir John Black some inspiration to follow the same course.

Although there can be no direct connection, on my regular visits to the Shanklin on the Isle of Wight the bus station in Landguard Road always reminds me of this stillborn venture. This interesting possibility, also found in the board meeting minutes, would have involved co-operation with Willys, who developed the original Jeep concept from the Bantam Car Company design for the US army in the Second World War, to make ready for mass production for the war effort.

Triumph Roadster, 1946–49

Finally, it is not possible to write this story without at least some mention in brief of the Triumph Roadsters, especially as the 1800 Saloon and Roadster were launched at the same time in 1946.

The profile of the Roadster was raised substantially with the maroon example, registration number J 1610, used in the long-running BBC TV series *Bergerac*, set in Jersey. However, with its long bonnet, driving on the narrow island roads might have been challenging, even

This Triumph Roadster wears the same Jersey registration number (J 1610) as the examples used in the popular *Bergerac* TV series, but did it really appear there?

Phase I Standard Vanguard.

for experienced drivers, when having to cope with their typical unforgiving roadside stone walls. I understand that more than one car was used in the series and that the sound effects from a TR sports car had to be dubbed on for effect!

A new version of the TV series has recently been filmed. By the time this book has been released it will have already been screened on the TV Channel U&Drama, and you know that the Roadster will indeed have a starring role once more as Jim Bergerac's car. I did read that the star of the original series, John Nettles, turned down the opportunity of taking on a cameo appearance in the new one.

Subsequently, the distinctive 1947 Standard Vanguard provided the power plant and drivetrain to the latter models, the 2000 Saloon and Roadster models, plus all the Renown models. At that time the USA led the world in car design, with many engineering firsts such as automatic gearboxes and even air-conditioning before the Second World War. American car design was to exert itself on so many British and European cars in the 1940s and 1950s, the Standard Vanguard being one early example, following the Jowett Javelin, with very different styling cues.

However, by complete contrast, the Triumph 1800 eschewed any American or European styling trends and could hardly be mistaken for anything other than a quintessentially British car.

Similarly, the small Razoredge Triumph Mayflower followed a broadly similar theme, also playing a part in the story too, therefore this model will also be covered briefly.

The First Triumph Cars History Book

I should pay tribute to the pioneering work by the late Richard Langworth (pre-war section) and the late Graham Robson (post-war section) in producing the first overall history of Triumph in the book *From 1923's Tri-car to the Acclaim: The Complete history of Triumph Cars*. It was initially published in 1979 (to mark the firm's seventy-five-year full history), then as a second edition in 1988 with a revised title after the car brand had been dropped, then again in 2018 when it was finally updated with some new colour photos. I should mention straightaway that Triumph motorbikes are still made in Britain – in the East Midlands.

It was wonderful to hear the story of the book's gestation from Richard himself at the Vintage Triumph Register Convention in Texas (back in 2016). I was very interested to know how this collaboration with Graham, from across the ocean, came about and, like many good ideas, it was all hatched in a pub – or in this case a bar, in London. Richard confirmed to me subsequently:

> We met at the bar of the Westland Hotel [still there] on Bayswater in 1976.
>
> He [Graham] had recently published *The Story of Triumph Sports Cars* (1973). And so I wrote with trepidation, the acolyte at the foot of Olympus. He couldn't have been kinder over my amateurish efforts.
>
> After I became a freelance, we met personally in London. There to my astonishment, he offered to co-author with me a complete history of our mutual passion. Triumph Cars, and to find us a publisher.

In the interest of fairness, I should add that, in common with Graham Robson, Richard's output of books can only be described as prolific, with fifty-four books to his credit, including those co-written, like the Triumph book. His credits cover not only automotive history, but also Winston Churchill. Added to this total are what must be countless articles published over the years along with his work as an editor of journals on his favourite subjects, including Packard cars. In 1998 he was awarded the CBE for 'his contributions to Anglo-American understanding and history'. His main base is in New Hampshire, USA.

An Earlier Book Only Covering Standard and Post-War Triumphs

This volume followed on from the late John Davy's much less detailed book on Standard Cars, which also covered post-war Triumphs: *The Standard Car 1903–63: An Illustrated History* published in 1967, which was an early source and possibly the only one at that stage to cover the entire years of SMC production. John had inside knowledge and access to official photos and records from his time working for SMC on the PR side.

I should mention that the major difference between the new book and the John Davy volume was that the authors obtained many first-hand accounts from the SMC personnel who were there at the time of production of the cars, a much less common practice at the time but now an essential ingredient of any motoring history book.

Triumph Car Marque Dropped by BL (Formerly British Leyland)

Soon after the first edition of the Langworth/Robson book came out, the sad end of the car marque was announced in *The Times* on 10 February 1984. It is hard to believe that its demise as a car brand is now over forty years ago, which is a length of time already over half as long as the Triumph Cars' complete history of making cars (excluding the war years when no Triumph cars were manufactured).

The centenary of the beginning of Triumph motor car production was celebrated in the summer of 2023 with an exclusively Triumph (and Standard) Cars Rally at Walton Hall, near Warwick (once owned by the late Danny La Rue), and a later event at Silverstone shared with MG – for so long rival marques, but in fact set up in the very same year. A Triumph from the first year of production – 1923 – attended this very nostalgic celebration of the marque, as did a few Standards as well.

Yet, as recently as 1973, and at a time when its fifty years in the car business was the subject of somewhat low-key celebrations, Triumph was building a very full range of models, including the attractive 2000 Mk II saloon and its estate car derivative. At the lower end of the scale was the Toledo and its more luxurious siblings, the 1500 TC and Dolomite saloons, while not forgetting the sporting Spitfire, TR6 and the top-of-the-range Stag models.

Triumph did, however, produce a fiftieth anniversary poster, which could be obtained by filling in a coupon in the local newspaper if there were a dealer in the vicinity. I did this at

The oldest surviving Triumph car, made in 1923, the first year of car production, at Walton Hall, Warwickshire, 2023.

MOTOR week ending May 5, 1973

50 YEARS ON

A special tribute to half a century of Triumph cars

In our issue of April 10, 1923, *The Motor* (as it then was) carried a full description of the first car—the 10hp tourer shown below—to be built by the old established Triumph company. At frequent intervals ever since we have been publishing descriptions and road tests of other new Triumphs.

In the following pages we look back at some earlier memorable Triumphs, and at their competition successes; we try a contemporary Triumph and find that it's almost the ideal long-distance touring car; and we look forward into the future of the company with its managing director, Bill Davis.

The front cover of *Autocar's 50 Years On* booklet.

the time, but I am still waiting for my copy! However, thanks to the generosity of Renown owner David Wickens, I did get my copy eventually many years later.

Anniversary articles appeared in both *Autocar* and *Motor* weekly magazines (long since merged as *Autocar*). The former produced a very informative and well-illustrated booklet to mark the anniversary.

The Italian designer Michelotti's influence on many of these designs should be highlighted here. At an Italian motor show a relationship was established with them and the late Harry Webster, despite neither party being able to speak a common language.

After the 1960 takeover of SMC, the then new owners Leyland Motors merged with British Motor Corporation (BMC) in 1968 to become the new British Leyland Motor Corporation Ltd (BLMC). Triumph was then to become part of the renamed BL and placed within that firm's Specialist Cars Division, along with Rover and Jaguar, which by then were also in its vast collection of car and commercial vehicle makes. It would have seemed unthinkable on that basis that the Triumph car marque would be consigned to history just eleven years after that fifty-year landmark.

Even worse for any Triumph enthusiast is that the last model produced was not even a 'true' Triumph, but a reworked or badge-engineered Honda Ballade made under licence. Consequently, it has no link to any previous model in its sixty-one-year history, apart from its brand name. I guess it gave the BL Group a ready-made last model to save any further development costs, but what a sad demise of a much-loved car brand back in 1984.

The former parent company brand, Standard, had expired previously in 1963. This was because by then the word 'standard' had changed over time to be regarded as 'basic', a major disadvantage if you were going to sell cars in the 1960s. Even the cheapest model in the range would now be branded as 'De Luxe', therefore the 'Standard' marque was dropped in this country.

However, somewhat bizarrely, the brand continued in India for another twenty-one years. Thus, on this basis, it even just outlasted its former senior stablemate, Triumph, in Britain. Models made there included a four-door Herald, marketed as the 'Standard Gazel' (*sic*). No four-door Herald was sold over here. The Indian marque lasted until 1985, when a much modified and somewhat boxy-looking Standard Atlas van, as production of the Standard 20, finally came to an end.

There have been many reports of a possible revival of the now BMW-owned Triumph marque, but not even a full-sized prototype has surfaced to my knowledge.

1

Sir John Black and the Acquisition of the Triumph Marque

No history of Standard or Triumph cars could ignore the influence and input of Sir John Black, the driving force behind SMC's progress before the Second World War and after it. Sir John Black has not been given a lot of credit in classic car press and books, but he was behind the rise – and possibly even the very survival – of Standard Motor Company, which was not in the best financial health when he joined it.

John Paul Black was born in Kingston, Surrey, in 1895. He was educated locally and studied law, which was no doubt a useful grounding for his later career. John was in the Royal Tank Regiment in the First World War and is known to have sustained injuries while serving his country in Ypres, Belgium, but I do not think they were ever identified at the time.

After the war, in 1918, he joined Hillman Cars and was very soon made a director at just twenty-four, but resigned after Rootes took over Hillman. In the meantime, he had married Daisy Hillman, but the marriage was dissolved in 1939. His brother-in-law was Spencer Wilks, later of Rover fame, who married another of the Hillman sisters.

Joining Standard in 1929, he soon became Joint MD in 1933, and then very quickly the sole MD when R. W. Maudslay died a year later. He led the firm through the Flying Standard era with much more streamlined cars that were directly influenced by the styling advances in the USA. This new design covered the full range of models from the Nine right up to the Twenty V8 version, and with a British engine too, and these models sold very well.

By 1939, Austin and Morris (then separate firms) had a total of 50 per cent of the British market, followed by Ford with 14.7 per cent, then SMC with 12.8 per cent (versus just 4.9 per cent in 1929). Note that Rootes Group, even with ownership of Hillman, Sunbeam and Humber, held only 11 per cent of the market, followed by Vauxhall with just 10.4 per cent, even with the might of General Motors behind it.

One of the defining decisions of the then government in the inevitable lead up to the Second World War was the establishment of duplicate factories, better known as 'shadow factories'. This was a very prescient decision because if there were to be a war city centres would most likely be targeted. Apart from the potential for loss of civilian life, many factories were located in city areas (a hangover from Victorian times and the Industrial

Sir John Black. (Courtesy of Nick Black)

Revolution) because workers tended to live near where they worked. Standard managed new shadow factories at Canley and Banner Lane, Coventry, for aero-engine production, facilities that would be at the heart of their road vehicle and tractor production later.

In 1943, John Black remarried, this time to Alicia Joan Linton. They had three sons together, of whom Nick Black survives and is based in the East Midlands.

The Second World War saw John Black play an essential part, this time (from July 1941) at top level as Chairman of the Joint Aero Committee, a role in which he was effective enough to earn a knighthood just two years later. However, he always preferred to be addressed as Captain Black in those more deferential times.

However, before the end of the Second World War he had already bought the rights to use the Triumph name, thus creating a ready-made more sporting and upmarket brand. New designs from Triumph Cars launched in early 1946, namely the 1800 Saloon and Roadster, followed later by the successful record-breaking TR2, which in turn led to a whole series of successor models.

Sir John also did very well to get the Ferguson Tractor project under his wing, making full use of the Banner Lane shadow factory facility. He must have backed his judgment when making the decision to authorise production of the very advanced looking, at least for 1947 Britain, Phase I Standard Vanguard. The Vanguard was a ground-breaking design and moreover had appeal beyond these shores in a way that earlier Standard cars had not done.

When the comparatively young Alick Dick was made MD in 1953, Sir John became Chairman. However, the following year, shortly after a serious accident, he was forced out of the company not long after this 'promotion'. Ironically, the accident involved a Standard works van. Sir John was a passenger, and it was caused by the driver trying to avoid a head-on collision. Not only this, but he was being driven in the TR2-based prototype or first-production Swallow Doretti sports car. It was driven by Ken Richardson, the heroic

The main entrance at Mallory Court, Leamington Spa, once the home of Sir John and his family and now a hotel.

driver of the record-breaking May 1953 TR2 runs on the Jabbeke Highway in Belgium, and this involved yet another prototype car.

Sir John died in 1965 and his well-attended memorial service in Coventry's then new cathedral included mourners from all levels of his former company which he had led for so many years. Nowadays, you can stay in one of the guest rooms (as I have done) in his former family home, Mallory Court in Leamington Spa, which is now a hotel.

The Acquisition of Certain Assets of the Former Triumph Car Company

In July 1939, the Triumph Motor Company went into receivership and the factory, equipment and goodwill were offered for sale. Then in September 1939, it was announced that the 'Goodwill & Assets of the Triumph Company of Coventry' had been acquired by the scrap merchants Thomas W Ward of Sheffield'.

While Thomas W. Ward had purchased Triumph, the effects of the Second World War again stopped the production of cars, and Triumph's Gloria and Stoke works in Coventry were very badly damaged during enemy action in 1940.

As a result, most of the company's records and assets were destroyed, along with so much of this formerly very attractive medieval city, as well as numerous other factories including those of Daimler, Humber-Hillman and machine tool makers Alfred Herbert Ltd.

Pre-war 'Globe' radiator badge.

Post-war 'Globe' radiator badge.

These raids on the city caused such an unprecedented and severe level of destruction that leading Nazi Joseph Goebbels later invented the word *coventriert* ('coventried') when describing similar levels of destruction in other British towns and cities.

In November 1944 what was left of the Triumph Motor Company and the Triumph trade name were bought by the Standard Motor Company and a new subsidiary, the Triumph Motor Company (1945) Limited, was formed, with future production transferred to Standard's factory at Canley, south of Coventry.

Very little, if anything, of Triumph's Coventry manufacturing facilities survived the war, but the transaction did include some land and presumably badly damaged buildings which were later all sold off. Therefore, crucially, the net price of the Triumph marque may have been relatively small. Included in the deal were the rights to use the 'Globe' badge and the 'Dolomite' model name, but apparently no other model names were sought. This was recorded in the very first board meeting minutes held at Briton Road in Coventry on 17 April 1945, with only Sir John Black and Mr C. J. Band listed as directors and Mr K. Aspland as Company Secretary. Sir John was immediately appointed both Chairman and Managing Director of the newly created firm.

Triumph's new owners had been supplying Standard engines and chassis to SS Cars Ltd. Soon after hostilities had ended SS Cars became Jaguar Cars Ltd due to the unfortunate connotations the previous name had acquired – incidentally, 'SS' had originally stood for 'Standard Swallow'.

Before the war Triumph had a totally different image from SMC, having largely made a range of sports cars and saloons, including the Dolomite, Gloria, Southern Cross and so on. Donald Healey worked in publicity for the firm, initially as experimental manager. He also rallied Triumphs, leading the publicity drive for his firm.

After an argument between Sir John and William Lyons, Black's objective was to build a car to compete with the soon to be launched post-war Jaguar after acquiring the rights to the name and the remains of the Triumph business. Even then, within the motor industry it was not unusual to have at least one 'companion marque' under an umbrella organisation, which was consistent with the large groupings in the USA such as General Motors and Chrysler.

Closer to home, by then Morris owned the Riley and Wolseley marques, while the Rootes Group, following the same practice, added Sunbeam and Humber to their stable of private car makes. The consistent strategy followed here was clearly to add upmarket brands to lower-priced, mass-produced makes to sell to a broader range of buyers (ideally with disposable wealth), especially younger buyers, as they would make their way up the ladder, inevitably gaining more experience and a greater salary.

Moving on to 1945 and the post-war car programme was starting to take shape. It was time to make some carefully crafted official leaks to a car-hungry public via the motoring press. For instance, in *The Autocar* issue of 23 February 1945 it was reported after the issue of an official press release:

> With the object of getting back into the production stride as soon as possible after the cessation of hostilities, the Standard Motor Co. Ltd has decided to concentrate on two up-to-date (Standard) models, an Eight of 1000cc and also a Twelve, It is proposed to produce a Ten hp Triumph of 1300cc and a Fifteen hp model of 1800cc.

Later, in the issue dated 30 March 1945, under the headline 'The New Triumph Cars, features of post-war Models Disclosed', the following announcement appeared:

> Prototypes of the Post-War cars show some interesting departures. Designed primarily to give lively performance, the cars are laid out to provide a maximum of seating accommodation, with an unusual degree of outward visibility for all passengers, and the driver, in particular. To that end, the door-pillars and screen pillars are exceptionally narrow. The styling is based on curved panels with relatively sharp edges.

That last feature, and many others, were especially relevant, as discussed below. Other features to be defined at this stage in the same article were:

- No sliding opening roof (typical of this class of car pre-war as it would save weight if deleted).
- Room for three people on the front seat – hence column gear change.
- Handbrake controlled by pistol grip.

It was also stated that 'the New Triumphs would have a very distinctive appearance' and that 'aluminium panels would be used'. This was a response to the steel shortage after the war and because aluminum was available in greater quantities than steel.

2

The Origins of the 'Razor-edge' School of Design

This appearance really goes back to the design of horse-drawn closed carriages. There was the need to use the maximum space within a short wheelbase, much like a box, and consequently one carriage was going to look much like another in most cases. I rather like the phrase the 'English Traditional School', as used by the late Virgil Exner to describe this type of design. He came up with this was after working at the top level in car styling in the USA after the war for both Studebaker and Chrysler. In particular, he enjoyed a heyday at the latter where his later 1950s designs were much 'cleaner' than many of his rivals.

A Hooper-bodied Rolls-Royce Silver Wraith.

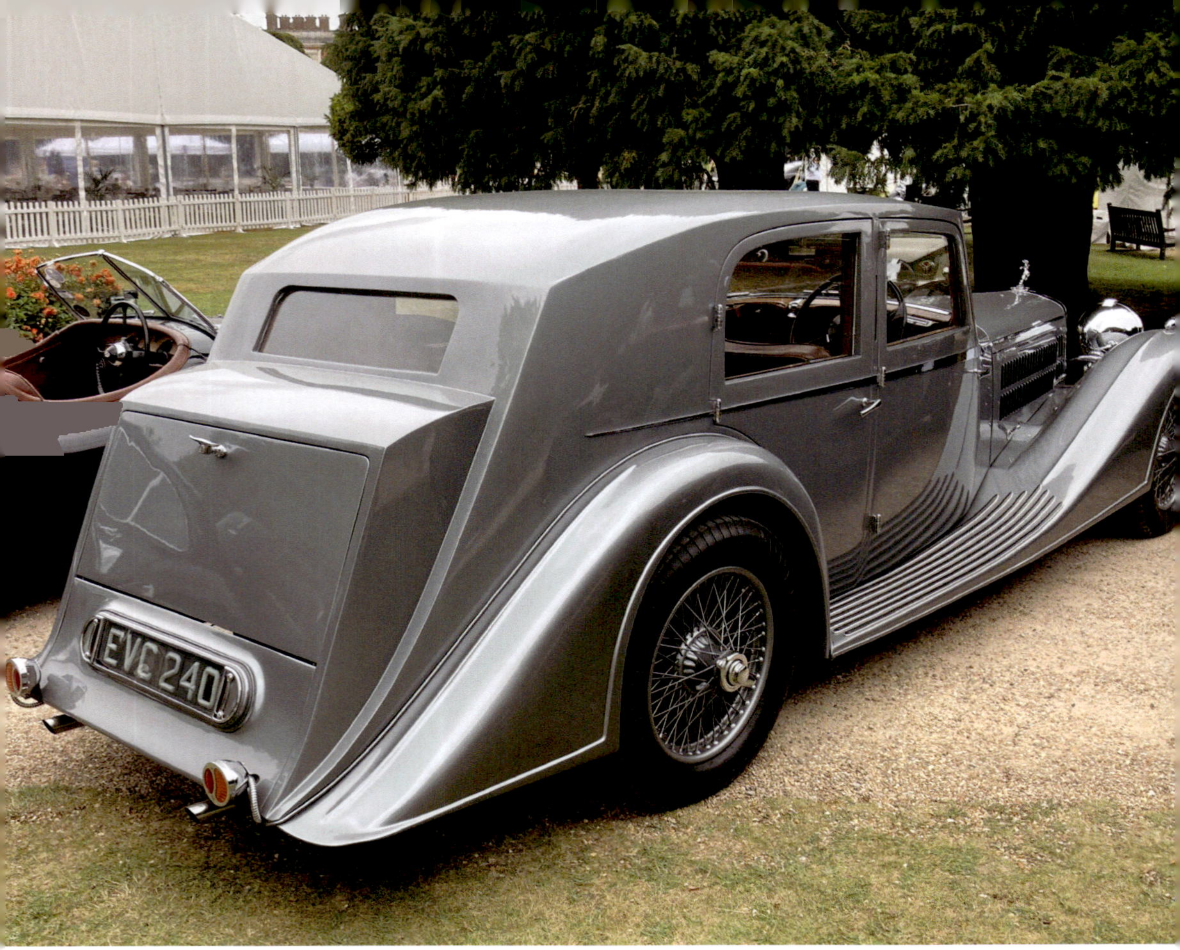

Above: A 1940 Alvis Speed Twenty-Five SC body by Van den Plas.

Left: A Packard Super Eight Town Sedan.

Pioneered in Britain by Freestone & Webb in the 1930s and often fitted to Rolls-Royce chassis, the look was very distinctive and later taken up by other firms, notably Hooper, well into the 1940s and after the war. Examples from Hooper were the 'Dauphin' Daimlers and some larger models feature razor-edge styling to a lesser or greater extent.

Indeed, the large Daimler Limousine and Hearses based on the Jaguar Mk X/420G platform (the DS420 model) continued that theme in an updated form right through to the end of production in 1992. The Armstrong Siddeley Sapphire was another proponent of the same general updated appearance for this, its last ever model, until it stopped making cars in 1960.

In slightly toned-down form, the style can be seen in the Rolls-Royce Silver Cloud and its twin, the Bentley S Type, manufactured from 1955 to 1966, when these models were replaced by the Silver Shadow and T-type respectively. The term 'knife-edge' was also used for a short time, but seems to have fallen into disuse after the 1950s.

Across the Atlantic there were examples too, notably on a Packard chassis. This was interesting to me as an enthusiast of that marque, especially as the British Hooper Company bodied at least one Super Eight Packard. Other examples on this American chassis were conceived and built locally.

The Development of the New 1800 Saloon and the Controversy

The 'father' of the design of the elegant 1800 Saloon will forever remain controversial. This is because two employees of Mulliners, Birmingham, were to claim credit in their unpublished memoirs – James Wignall and Leslie (Les) Moore. I was not able to meet either gentleman, but I almost met the late Les Moore in Cornwall after the family moved here from the West Midlands following his retirement from Triumph Cars in British Leyland days. However, Les did make an attractive wooden model in 1949 as a possible replacement concept for the then current 2000 Saloon but with much more modern styling. I was allowed to photograph it thanks to the late Keith Jay, nephew of Louis Antweiler, MD of Mulliners, Birmingham.

Les was only tracked down when he spotted TROC member Brian Murrish's 2000 Saloon near his home in Truro and declared to an astonished Brian: 'I designed that car!' When news of this story reached me, I arranged to see Les Moore and family in Cornwall. He very sadly died just beforehand, but his widow and Chris still saw me on the appointed date and kindly gave me a copy of his unpublished autobiography.

We shall never know the true story, of course, but it is only fair to mention that James Wignall's version was corroborated by the late Stuart Peck (also from Mulliners), whom I was to meet many times. Stuart designed the beautiful Mulliner-bodied Bentley Mk VI convertible, registration number JPB 2, which was re-imported to this country only relatively recently. I was lucky enough to see this vehicle unexpectedly for the first time in Essex in 2019 after its long American sojourn. This was the very last traditional coach-built car by Mulliners, who then concentrated on conversion work, often for SMC, as well as bus and coach body building before being bought by SMC.

Above and below: The beautifully made 1949 wooden model by Les Moore during his time at Mulliners of Birmingham.

The 1952 Bentley Mk VI Drophead Foursome Coupé, built by Mulliners of Birmingham specifically for Sir John Black, JPB 2.

I should also mention that while it is understood that the former Triumph pre-war design chief Walter Belgrove (but then in a similar post in SMC) would have signed off the Triumph Razoredge design, his only contribution was to add a bevel to the bottom of the rear fixed side window. It was a clever styling feature nevertheless, but the car clearly owed nothing else to his design skills. Indeed, my good friend and TROC colleague Tom Robinson visited him in retirement in Devon in a Razoredge car with owner Brian Murrish in the 1980s, but when Belgrove saw the car he declared immediately that 'he never did like those cars', leaving both Tom and the poor Triumph owner somewhat open-mouthed. A case of 'not invented here syndrome' perhaps? However, much to their relief, they were soon invited in for 'tea and banana sandwiches' and at least they were offered the choice between Indian and Chinese tea!

It is clear from my research, including a trawl through his archives courtesy of the Coventry Motor Museum, that Walter Belgrove took his styling influences from the other side of the Atlantic Ocean, notably Detroit. Walter Belgrove was appointed Head of Design at the then independent Triumph Motor Company in Coventry in 1935, and in those archives I found a series of front-end photographs, all taken by him at a late 1930s Earls Court Motor Show comprising only American cars.

Sure enough, the 1937 Vitesse and Dolomite Saloon and Roadster had very attractive 'English styling', coupled with the option of a Detroit-designed Hudson-esque waterfall radiator grille (or 'Fencer's mask' – both terms were used).

The demise of the original Triumph Car company in July 1939 had ended in bankruptcy, despite its history of making both stylish large and small cars (its smallest – the Super 7 – was about the size of an Austin 7) since 1923. However, the Triumph motorcycle business continued after having already been sold off in in 1936, and of course it still does today.

Back in 1946, Britain had just fought and won a hugely expensive war, both in terms of lives and resources, and the country was in very poor shape financially. Indeed, this 'war debt' owed to the USA was not paid off in full, including interest, until as recently

Above left: A 1937 Hudson Terraplane – note the 'Waterfall' radiator grille.

Above right: Triumph's take on that design.

Below: A Triumph Dolomite Roadster – a wonderful Walter Belgrove design.

as 2006. Much of the industrial fabric of the Midlands and elsewhere had been destroyed and peacetime production of consumer products, including cars, was underway again after many years of war work.

Raw material shortages were the norm and, along with all the problems of rebuilding industry after the war, when the focus had to be on manufacturing war materiel, the whole structure of virtually every company had also to be recreated as employees were returning to peacetime work.

The Influence of Sir John

We know that Sir John Black liked razor-edge styled cars and was certainly directly connected with the shape and conception of a new SS Jaguar saloon, which was built by Mulliners Ltd of Bordesley Green, Birmingham, a totally separate firm from the better-known H. J. Mulliner.

That car was described in *The Autocar* dated 30 June 1939, and it was said to be a present for his wife. It was stated that it could also have had 'marketing possibilities'. Indeed, so pleased was Sir John with this car that a second car was to be built, but it seems most unlikely that it was constructed. Nevertheless, one car – registration ERW 470 – duly appeared, and the body was based on a design prepared by Mulliners for Mr Antweiler's Rolls-Royce, which Sir John had admired.

I wonder if Sir John felt that it was more appropriate for him to run a Jaguar, rather than a Rolls-Royce or Bentley, as SS cars bought components from Standard pre-war? From the rear the car looked vaguely like a post-war Bentley Mk VI or an Austin Princess. It was perhaps less distinctive from the front, with an unhappy combination of curvy front wings and radiator grille of the Jaguar contrasting with the razor-edge coach-built body. While reported as a collaboration between Louis Antweiler, Managing Director of Mulliners, and Black, the car was designed by their draughtsmen under James Wignall. Sadly, this attractive car was reported to have been cut up as long ago as 1954.

The Prototype Triumph 1800 Saloon

Post-war, the 1800 was to be a further collaboration between Standard and Mulliners. Before 1800 commenced production, a prototype was constructed. Vic Hammond, then a tool designer at Standard before later becoming an accomplished stylist, takes up the story:

> My knowledge of the Renown and Roadster started in 1945 when I was given the job of designing assembly jigs for the Roadster at Canley, Coventry ... I can well remember when I moved to work at Banner Lane, Tile Hill, Coventry where we had set up one of the first styling studios, if not the first, in the UK. The first Razoredge Triumph was created by Mulliners at Bordesley Green, Birmingham now extinct, from directions given by Sir John Black to an émigré Belgian called Louis Antweiler, the owner of Mulliners and his MD Lt. Colonel White, ostensibly as a Post-War car for them to produce, for SMC (Standard Motor Company) — the body that is.

The direction given was to sharpen up the profile of the pre-war Standard 12/14 body. I think the car was eventually acquired by the late E.G. (Ted) Grinham, then to Harry Webster.

Certainly, having met the late Harry Webster at his home in Kenilworth, he confirmed that he had indeed owned the car and kindly allowed me to borrow his photos for scanning. However, he confirmed that Grinham ran the car only on test runs in considerable secrecy, often at night, for Standard and did not own the car. Harry Webster told me that he had been the first owner after the factory. However, this version was not an entirely successful design, with its 100-inch wheelbase (vs 108 inch for the 1800) and a very unfortunate 'Flying Standard' style boot. This prototype was built during 1945.

A Revised Design – Now Closer to the Production Version of 1800

Sir John Black did not like it either and ordered the design to be improved. He usually got what he wanted and, of course, he was right. The design was indeed considerably improved. The design deficiencies were corrected since it had been clearly too short and stubby.

A 1945 Triumph 1800 short-wheelbase saloon – note Flying Standard boot treatment.

The next stage we reach in the story is the manufacture of a pre-production prototype of the now longer car, probably during the second half of 1945. This revised vehicle was photographed wearing trade plates against the background of stone walls, possibly a castle and almost certainly in Warwickshire, not far south of the Coventry factories.

The differences between the production version and this one-off are relatively few, but noticeable once you look closely at this early version, e.g.:

- Side lights lower down the front wings (not on top).
- Door handles have oval escutcheons.
- Starting handle guide on bumper more substantial.
- Different fuel cap assembly on rear wing.
- Different door hinges on 'B post'.
- No running board strips.

The new 1800 broke new ground in several ways, but especially because it was a mass-produced (relatively speaking) coach-built Razoredge saloon, and obtainable within a similar price band to a Rover saloon.

Standard Motor Company Before the Triumph Purchase

As Managing Director of Standard, John Black had helped to build up the company from a relatively small concern to one of the 'Big Six' manufacturers of mass-produced cars – the British Austin, Morris, Rootes Group and Standard, along with American-owned Ford and the General Motors subsidiary Vauxhall.

Standard produced a series of solid cars, their fortunes changing with the launch of their new Flying Standard cars, originally (in prototype form) owing something to the revolutionary Chrysler Airflow – a radically streamlined car – launched in Detroit in 1934, which was to influence manufacturers from Sweden (Volvo) to Japan (Toyota's first car) – and in Britain, in the shape of the Singer Airstream.

The Airflow contrasted dramatically with the largely two-box look of almost every other contemporary car on the road at the time, as would the Vanguard in Britain later. Meanwhile, in Coventry, the new Flying Standard was made in various forms from the small 8-hp model to the larger 16, all initially having a sloping back. There was even a V8 version: the Flying Twenty. In October 1936 this introduced an even more streamlined look, with a new waterfall radiator grille later used, in modified form, for the whole range. This new grille design, topped by the Union Flag, though not as extreme as those of the Belgrove-designed Triumphs, did have a generally similar outline.

The 1936 model Plymouth, part of the Chrysler Corporation, had already introduced a very similar grille from the autumn of 1935. Plymouth was a new marque (originally launched as the Chrysler Plymouth from 1928) designed to compete at the lower end of the pricing scale with Ford and GM's Chevrolet marques. The ship the *Mayflower* reputedly made land at Plymouth Rock in Massachusetts in 1620 and the connection was reinforced by the makers to include a stylised 'Mayflower' mascot on the grille's top. By coincidence, the Triumph Mayflower had the very same device some thirteen years later.

Above: A 1936 Plymouth 'Mayflower' radiator mascot.

Left: A Mayflower bonnet catch-cum-mascot.

3

The Different Triumph Razoredge Models

For clarity, I feel I should now set out the salient details of the five different models to make the text easier to absorb later, before providing more information about each variation in subsequent chapters. However, first, I should reiterate that within Standard-Triumph, 'Commission Number' is the equivalent of Chassis Number or today's VIN Number.

Each model had a prefix, in letters, to indicate the relevant model; for example, 'V' for Vanguard. The prefix for Triumph models started with the letter 'T', as in 'TD' for 1800 Saloon, 'TDA' for 2000 Saloon, etc.

Triumph 1800 Saloon – Commission Number Prefix: TD (Produced 1946–49)

- 1,776cc Triumph four-cylinder engine. Tubular chassis, Girling hydraulic brakes on all four wheels. Four-speed column change with right-hand control. Transverse leaf front suspension.
- Light alloy and steel body over ash frame. Alloy boot, doors and bonnet lids. Steel wings. All these body features are common to the five variations.
- Roadster-style nave plates (hubcaps) with 'Globe' centres.
- Exhaust exits from the nearside – the sole variation to do so.

Triumph 2000 Saloon – Commission Number Prefix: TDA (Produced Only for a Few Months in 1949)

- Now with a 2,088cc four-cylinder Vanguard engine. Tubular chassis. Three-speed Vanguard gearbox column change, but still the right-hand control of its predecessor. Transverse leaf front suspension.
- Externally almost identical to the 1800 Saloon.
- Exhaust pipe exits from the offside, like all subsequent models.

All five Razoredge variations, though I cheated slightly since David Shulver's 1800 Saloon (second left) had to stand in for an absent 2000 Saloon.

Triumph Renown – Commission Number Prefix: TDB (Produced 1949–51)

- The first to be given a permanent model name.
- 2,088cc four-cylinder Vanguard engine, box section chassis, independent suspension, Lockheed hydraulic brakes on all four wheels. Three-speed gearbox, now with left-hand control.
- Revised dashboard with rectangular dials. Smaller headlamps. New, more substantial, bumpers and overriders. New radiator mascot introduced after initial models lacked this feature. Overdrive gearbox made available later from June 1950.
- Vanguard-type nave plates (hubcaps) with 'Globe' centres.
- Exhaust pipe exits from the offside.

Triumph Renown (Long Wheelbase) – Commission Number Prefix: TDC (Produced 1952–54)

- Similar to TDB Renown in overall appearance, but with 3-inch longer wheelbase, new air vent on bulkhead in front of windscreen, push button door handles. Wider rear window.

Triumph Renown Limousine (Long Wheelbase) Commission Number Prefix: TDC Plus Suffix LIM (Produced 1951–54)*

- Externally identical to the TDC Renown. Fixed front bench seat. Fixed division with sliding window.
- A radio and heater were provided as standard.

**NB: The Commission Number had a lettered suffix too: 'DL' for De Luxe, though there were no 'basic' models produced. In subsequent parts of this book I ignore this aspect, except where the suffix is 'LIM'. Triumph Mayflowers used the prefix 'TT' and for the TR2 it was 'TS'.*

4

The 1800 Triumph Saloon – TD Prefix

Launched soon after the war, in 1946, the 1800 Saloon soon seemed to lose its original 'Town & Country' moniker very quickly. Aside from being a bit of a mouthful, it may not have been used for other reasons as set out below.

Chrysler, in the USA, had already introduced a very different 'Town & Country' motorcar of their own in 1941/2. This was a 'woody station wagon' yet with a steeply curved rear aspect, rather like a saloon. Post-war, they also used the same model name for a 'woody convertible' initially (and many other lesser vehicles over many subsequent years).

I wonder if this was why the Triumph model name was changed in order to avoid potential problems with Chrysler, who used the model name first on a 'luxury station wagon' and then many other lesser vehicles over subsequent years.

The 1800 Saloon was coach built by Mulliners of Birmingham, having aluminium doors, plus boot lid and bonnet and scuttle, a wood-faced dashboard with lots of wood cappings, fine carpet, leather upholstery and a quality woollen headlining. This was a very luxurious package in 1946, and all for under £1,000 inclusive of tax! You even got four forward speeds too. Interestingly, the Triumph 1800 Roadster (announced at the same time) was referred to as '1800 Coupé' in early advertising material – another name that was very short-lived.

Motor Panels (Coventry) Ltd, known locally as 'Coventry Motor Panels', built the steel bodies, including wings, for Triumph, as was confirmed much later, though they would have thence been transported to coachbuilders Mulliners for finishing, who were based in Bordesley Green, east of Birmingham. Presumably the Coventry firm also constructed the aluminium doors, boot lid and bonnet covers.

This Mulliner coachbuilding firm was an entirely different firm from H. J. Mulliner, later Mulliner Park Ward (now owned by Rolls-Royce), not to be confused with the Northampton-based Arthur Mulliner.

Apart from an anonymous body number on the bulkhead, under the bonnet there was nothing, not even a doorplate, to show on any of these cars that they were bodied by Mulliners. I always thought that it was odd that 'Coachwork by Mulliners of Birmingham Ltd' was not used by Standard-Triumph as an obvious selling point, such as in its advertising campaign, but in fairness neither Alvis nor Daimler drew attention to this connection for their Fourteen or Consort saloons respectively.

The Launch of the New Model

The Autocar for 14 February 1946 revealed that the first two cars of the new Triumph range, the 1800 Saloon and Roadster, had been shipped to Zurich for the display in the Congress Hall there as part of a show of Standard and Triumph cars organised by the local distributor, AMAG.

Interestingly, at the same time Sir John Black drew attention to the development of a new Standard model, which was being 'developed and tested for World conditions'. Of course, this was later launched as the Standard Vanguard, which was to play a very important part in the history of both brands. The Vanguard would replace all the remaining examples of the Flying Standard cars produced in the early post-war years.

Triumph was not the first company to introduce a new range of cars post-war, however. Both Armstrong-Siddeley and Riley had announced their new model ranges even before the end of 1945, but these tended to be exceptions when most manufacturers merely re-launched mildly

The 1800 looks good from any angle, even from above. (Courtesy Bernhard Ruest)

modified pre-war models, just as Standard did. All three companies did incredibly well to be able to do so, bearing in mind the end of hostilities was officially recorded as 2 September 1945 and London had experienced its final V2 rocket attack in March of that year.

The first production car, as opposed to the prototype or pre-production (pilot run) 1800 Saloons, Commission Number TD 1, was produced on 18 April 1946. Upon introduction in March 1946, prices were as follows:

Saloon	£650 + purchase tax	£831 6*s.* 1*d.* in all (£831.30)
Roadster	£625 + purchase tax	£797 7*s.* 3*d.* in all (£797.36)

In case these seem like a bargain, if updated to 2024 prices the tax-inclusive values equate to £29,205 (Saloon) or a mere £28,010 for the Roadster.

Bernhard Ruest's 1800 Saloon makes a great contrast with the construction machinery behind. (Courtesy Bernhard Ruest)

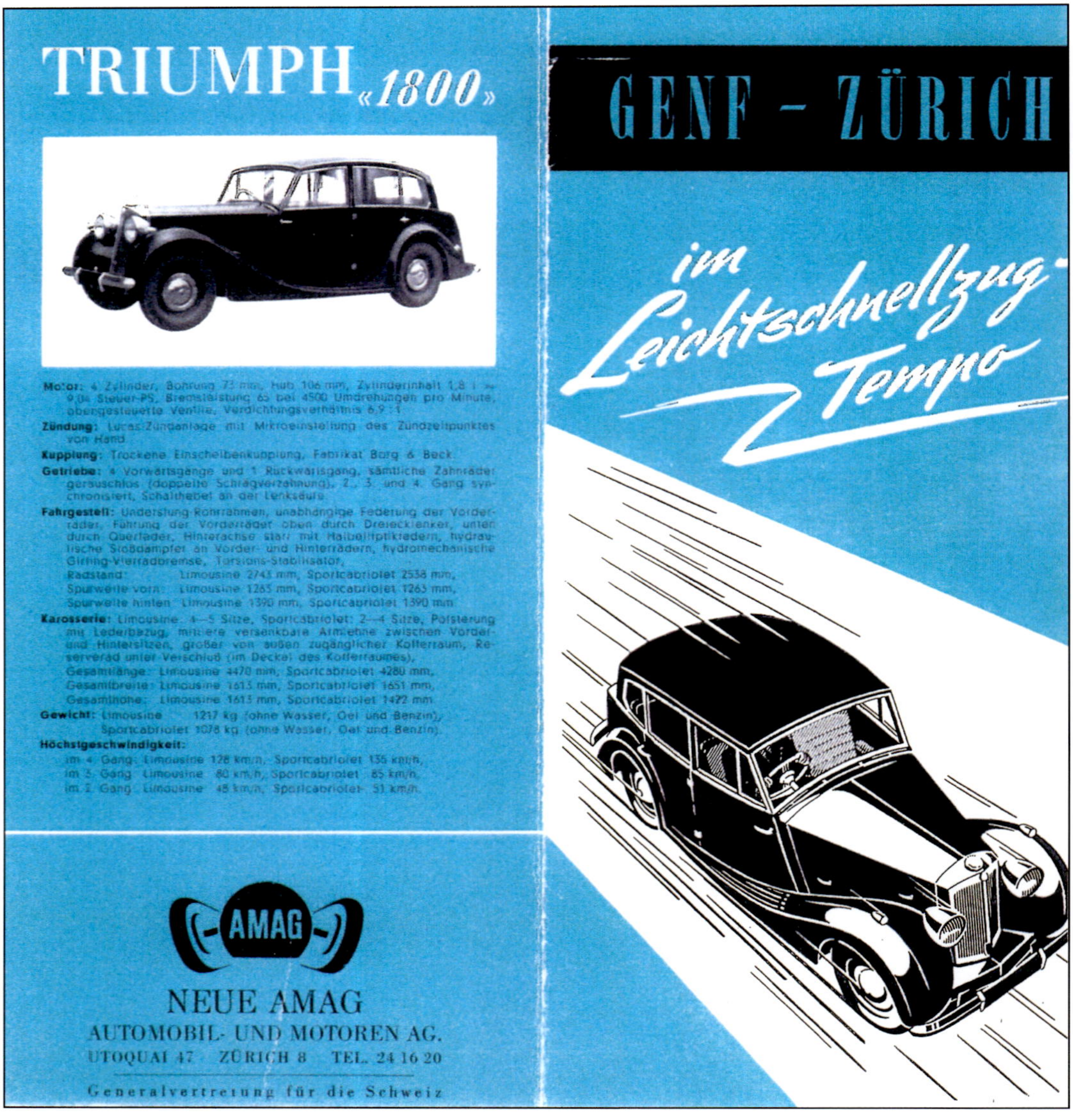

A facsimile of a German 1800 brochure.

In May 1947, the two cars were priced at £775 plus tax, illustrating the effect of inflation at the time, a process that has continued to ensure that the British pound has lost 98 per cent of its value since then!

At first glance there is little to connect the traditional look of the 1800 with any newfangled ideas imported from over the Atlantic; that is, however, until you sit inside and note the bench seat and column gearchange on the right of the steering column, a feature continued with the successor 2000 models. It was also consistent with the equivalent Roadster models too. However, regardless of whether specified with right-hand or left-hand control, these 1946 models were still the first British cars to have any form of column change.

A nice shot of a fleet of 1800 Saloons in St Peter Port, Guernsey. (TROC archives)

The chrome window frames were a distinctive feature too, reminiscent of the 1938 Cadillac Sixty special. The bench-type form seat was a new feature and generally associated with later post-war cars.

Incidentally, in my (admittedly biased) opinion, the updated Razoredge design was a much more modern take on that established pre-war styling feature.

The 'six light' (three side windows) gave the cabin a very light and airy feel, especially when compared with pre-war cars. While this view can only be subjective, I believe that many people would accept that the overall design on the slightly longer 9-foot, or 108-inch, wheelbase looked very attractive from every angle.

The most striking feature of the 1800 Saloon, apart from its distinctive 'Razoredge' look, were the slim window pillars and 'B-post' – the central (aluminium) post from which the doors were attached. These characteristics gave the car a very light and airy appearance inside, which was often favourably commented at the time. Indeed, you need only to sit in almost any pre-war saloon car to see what I mean.

Writer George Robbins, in his book *Coachwork*, commented on the styling: 'Its main body shape was an interesting combination of gentle curves and straight lines, with which the bold sweep and decisive shape of its mudguard contrasted effectively.' Personally, I do not think this could have been put any more accurately.

To bring the story up to date, 2024 was notable for the discovery of the oldest-surviving large Razoredge saloon. It was located by Bernhard Ruest, in Switzerland, some seventy-eight years after it was made. This is TD 2, the second production car, and I should add that the full story of this remarkable survivor has still to be told.

TD 2, the oldest surviving 1800 and Razoredge saloon in the world, discovered in Switzerland in 2024. (Courtesy of Herr Roscher of Roscher Classic)

5

The 2000 Saloon – TDA Prefix

The year 1949 was to prove an eventful one for Standard-Triumph, especially after the introduction of the ground-breaking Standard Vanguard with the so-called 'Beetle Back', which seemed to owe nothing to any other British car on the road at the time.

This year was also a significant one for Triumph: the 1800 Saloon had been replaced by the 2000 Saloon, the 2000 Roadster continued for a few more months, and later that year two significant Triumphs were launched – the smaller Razoredge 'Mayflower' companion car and the 'Renown' itself.

This Vanguard model now replaced the 'Flying Standard' series of cars, which were only mildly updated after the war. SMC were easily able to sell these vehicles due to pent-up demand.

Indeed, in contemporary postcards showing street views it is very easy to recognise the Vanguard, standing out among rows of mainly 'two-box' cars then on the road. Its all-enveloping bodywork also made a huge contrast with the more traditional Razoredge Triumphs of every type. However, it was certainly inspired by an American design, and this is where the American marque 'Plymouth' enters the story again.

The late John Davy, formerly working for SMC in Coventry, had written in his book about a sketch made surreptitiously by Walter Belgrove, at Sir John's request, of a 1942 model Plymouth sedan outside the American embassy, then in Grosvenor Square, Central London. But this sketch was not shown in the book and had always intrigued me. Long before the sketch went on general display in the Coventry Motor Museum, on a plaque in front of their Vanguard, I was privileged to see the original sketch when I was allowed to view the Belgrove Archives. It was a moment I will never forget.

However, returning to the story, it was now time to update the mechanical specification of the 1800 Saloon to produce the new 2000 Saloon and its stablemate, the 2000 Roadster (with a TRA Commission Number prefix), using a much more up-to-date largely Vanguard-based drivetrain. That Vanguard 2,088cc engine – or modified versions of thereof – was to power thousands of Ferguson TE 20 tractors (the so-called 'little Grey Fergies'), as well as Morgans, Triumph TRs and other sports cars.

The origins of the 1800 Saloon's drivetrain were to some extent pre-war, so now this style was accompanied by a modern mechanical specification.

Above: A rare contemporary view of a 1949 Comet Blue 2000 Saloon. (Courtesy of David Siddom – seen as a baby with his mother)

Below: 2000 Saloon KXB 149 at the inaugural TROC Rally in 1976.

A 1949 shot of the productions line, evidenced by this view of Roadster, 2000 Saloon and Vanguard models. (Courtesy of Coventry Archives)

The first 2000 Saloon – and remember, the Renown was to come later in the year – was constructed at Canley, Coventry, as commission No. TDA 1 on 9 February 1949, prior to the launch to the public in March.

In mid-1949, it is known that 220 cars were produced, if you take the example of a single day, which comprised 200 Vanguards plus ten TRA Roadsters and ten TDA 2000 Saloons.

Only 2,000 copies of the new car were officially made, but thanks to some sterling work carried out by Phil Homer of the Standard Motor Club, who combed through surviving production records, it is now known that a couple more examples left the factory. The last TDA 2002 was produced on 24 October 1949, though another source states that TDA 2000 was built slightly later, on 3 November 1949. The last 2000 Roadster was made not long before this, on 19 September 1949 – a grey car with a grey interior. Of these, ninety-one were exported; by comparison, 2,000 'Roadsters' (with the 2,088cc Vanguard unit) were also built.

I know from experience that combing through production records is very time-consuming, as you are searching through pages and pages of cars that might not have the same appeal as the specific models you might be looking for.

The 2000 was only made for a few months because there was a third Razoredge model also about to be launched in this year, described below, as well as the companion 'small car' also with a similar theme – the new Mayflower, on which so many hopes were built by the makers. I cover this model briefly in a later chapter as even to this day it is so closely linked to, and frequently confused with, the larger Razoredge cars covered in this book. In terms of numbers, the Mayflower outnumbered its close relative by about a ratio of 2:1 on a shorter production run. By contrast, it is interesting to note that 2,501 1800 Roadsters had been built while 4,000 production 1800 Saloons left the factory.

Instead of the more orthodox left-hand shift, this new 2000 Saloon retained its predecessor's unique (i.e. for a right-hand-drive car) right-hand gear change, still column mounted of course, linked to a Vanguard three-speed gearbox and Vanguard back axle. Mechanically, though, apart from the new Vanguard drivetrain, the 2000 Saloon had more in common with the 1800 than the Renown. The same applied to its external and internal appearance.

The new car started with the transverse front spring set-up, with suitably modified tubular chassis (to take the new drivetrain) of the earlier car. The bumper blades and overriders, hubcaps and headlights were all similar to before, as were internal fitments including circular instrument dials, rear blind (to cover its rear window) and seats. The smaller 10-gallon fuel tank was kept, along with Girling Hydrastatic (hydraulic) brakes.

Thus the 2000 Saloon was really something of a hybrid, in the original sense of the word, of course – a kind of halfway stage in the development of the Renown from the original 1800 Saloon. Owners of a 2000 Saloon or a 2000 Roadster will search in vain for a workshop manual for their car. A handbook was produced, along with a parts list, but these were both shared with the Roadster.

The Vanguard in Brief

It has been demonstrated that the Vanguard was a ground-breaking British design. Even its engine size, at over 2 litres, was rather larger than most of its Flying Standard predecessors and many of its rivals, which were typically fitted with engines of only about 10 hp or 1,100cc.

Early Vanguards were fitted with a smaller 1,849cc engine, and the right-hand column change of the TD and TDA Saloons (and Roadsters) persisted. But changes were soon made to increase the capacity to 2,088cc, with the gear change control placed in the expected position – to the left of the steering column.

The new car was a genuine attempt to create what would now be called a 'world car', exactly as Sir John envisaged, to assist the then Labour government's 'Export or Die' campaign to earn much-needed foreign currency for the country. A typical pre-war-built car from any major British manufacturer was designed for the home market and if overseas sales resulted then this was a bonus, especially if it came from beyond the British Empire.

It should be noted that the Vanguard would have a better chance of competing with American imports to the likes of South Africa, Australia and New Zealand, where a typically British 10-hp car would be totally unsuitable for long journeys in those vast countries. The Vanguard's advanced appearance – for conservative British tastes of the time – was promoted by Sir John Black and was a huge gamble looking back on it.

By contrast, if you take the new 1949 Rover 'Cyclops' saloon, also launched in 1949, this car, which was inspired by a very different post-war American car design, drew much criticism in

A superb example of a Standard Vanguard.

the motoring press from its traditional-minded clientele at the time. As with the Vanguard, the Rover 75 was then the sole saloon car being made by that company. Viewed through a twenty-first-century lens, the Vanguard now looks much too short and stubby, especially when compared, say, with the Rover 75, simply because it was about a foot shorter than the Renown, but it was a major styling advance and its landmark design is often overlooked.

Contrasting rear ends: Phase I Vanguard to the left and Phase II to the right.

6

The Renown Arrives – TDB Prefix

The Renown was now the third variation of the large Razoredge design to be made, in a year when the last 1800 versions were still being produced in modest numbers, with the 2000 version following it.

Neither of the earlier 1946–49 cars are really 'Renowns', even though all three models looked much the same externally, but underneath the body and in the cabin was a very different story.

It is not surprising there is confusion with these earlier cars, as the Marketing Department seems to have had second thoughts about what to call this latest model. Note that this was even after the official launch in the autumn of 1949, ahead of the annual Earls Court Motor Show, in London – only the second such show after the war.

The commission number plate says '2000', but it is taken from a 1951 Renown.

You might well wonder, like me, why this model, with all its major changes, does not have the 'Renown' name anywhere on the car – inside or out. Even the circular under-bonnet alloy plate, which carries the Commission Number, shows 'Triumph 2000' and not 'Triumph Renown'. But that was not even the name it was given initially, so the circular plate was never updated, even after a new model name was applied.

Clearly, as a much updated 'new' model, it needed to be distinguished from the earlier 2000, but, bizarrely, it was initially going to be called the 'Triumph 2 Litre Saloon'; however, even in a pre-decimal Britain that would hardly seem a lot different from the predecessor '2000 Saloon' to many people.

Brochures and such were prepared showing this somewhat low-key new name. In one November issue of the best-selling motoring magazine of the time, this new name was confirmed in an advertisement for the 'Big Announcement'. But someone in Triumph must have had second thoughts about the negligible impact the launch could have on the public with such a moniker, especially when the firm's PR effort was mainly directed towards launching the Mayflower with as much fanfare and ballyhoo as the company could muster. I can imagine why that exposure would befit a car like the Mayflower, made specifically with export markets in mind and, in common with the Vanguard launched in 1948, also expected to earn valuable foreign currency. I say this because the near identical advert in the following week's issue magically transformed from '2-Litre' to 'Renown' for the first time:

- 18 November 1949: Reference to the '1950 2-Litre Triumph Saloon'.
- 25 November 1949: Reference to the '1950 2-Litre Triumph Renown'.

By contrast, the launch of the Renown had been a very low-key affair, especially for a top-of-the-range vehicle. True, it did not look that different from the predecessor 2000 Saloon. While the Vanguard driveline was retained, there were many other differences, as will be discussed below.

TDB 1–3 were all built in October 1949, just before the last 2000 Saloon was made on 3 November 1949. TDB 4 appeared on 4 November 1949, after which production got underway. By July 1950, Renowns were being produced at around twenty per day, with Vanguards coming out at a rate of 170 per day, and Mayflowers 100 per day.

Key New Features

Early on in the TDB production run, the panelling of the leather on the seats was altered; at the rear, no doubt to the relief of non-smokers, the side ashtrays were eliminated.

What were the main differences between Renown and its forerunner? It is probably easier to list them, although the immediately noticeable external differences were the smaller 7-inch Lucas headlamps and different bumpers and overriders, the latter being identical to the Mayflower, whose section the bumpers shared. Other features were Vanguard hubcaps but with the Triumph 'Globe'; different steering and brakes; new, independent front suspension with coil springs; Vanguard-style box section chassis instead of tubular; left-hand column gear change; new instrument panel with Vanguard-style rectangular gauges; and detail differences in interior fittings.

STJ 782 crosses Tissington Ford when owned by Tom Robinson. It is now the property of his cousin, Robert Ward, in Derbyshire.

Initially, the prestigious showroom brochures similarly sported the new name (i.e. '2-Litre Saloon') until, presumably, the next print run when 'Renown' would be substituted. The main drawing in the brochure for the brand-new car even showed the wrong headlamps and nave plates, however. There was presumably nothing in the budget to add, say, Renown badging in or script anywhere on the bodywork or inside the car. No wonder most non-car enthusiasts regularly ask what it is!

Some minor alterations were made in 1950: the instrument panel was changed from featuring a black dial with cream and green markings and cream pointers to black dials with off-white and white markings and white pointers. This was implemented from TDB 3454, but just three, T0B 3461–3, oddly reverted to the green style.

As mentioned before, the main changes were out of sight for the casual passerby, so it is little wonder that the previous models were retrospectively (and incorrectly) renamed 'Renown' by many enthusiasts not familiar with these minutiae and the model history. Indeed, just look at auction website ads for the wonderful Dinky 1800 Saloon scale model, which is often advertised under 'Triumph Renown' and not '1800 Saloon', as described on the baseplate.

The seats were still a bench style at the front, which could just about take three, thanks to the absence of the usual floor change gearstick.

Just eighty-eight cars were constructed during the last few weeks of 1949, with only one car built on some days while production took time to ramp up. TDBs 6 and 7/8 were all completed on 21 and 22 November 1949 respectively.

Above and right: The immaculate and inviting interior of TDB Renown WHX 301. (Courtesy of Mike Sampson)

Overdrive Introduced as an Optional Extra

In 1950 the Laycock de Normanville Overdrive system was available for both the Renown and Vanguard at extra cost. It was perhaps the most significant change during production of the first TDB series Renowns. This optional accessory involved a chassis alteration from Renown TDB 3001, so that any subsequent vehicle could receive the new Overdrive box. It improved fuel consumption and transformed the smoothness of the vehicle considerably.

Both cars were the first cars to use this device, which transformed the driving experience, as I can also testify, having had one fitted to my car a few years after the original purchase with manual (cable) control, which worked very effectively provided you kept accelerating. It was controlled mechanically by pulling the gear lever towards you. Later in production, in January 1954, electrically controlled Overdrive was available, and this would be on the later TDC model. The mechanism on my own car worked on the third (top) gear only without the need to de-clutch, and if you did accidently take your foot off the throttle there was a disturbing clunk.

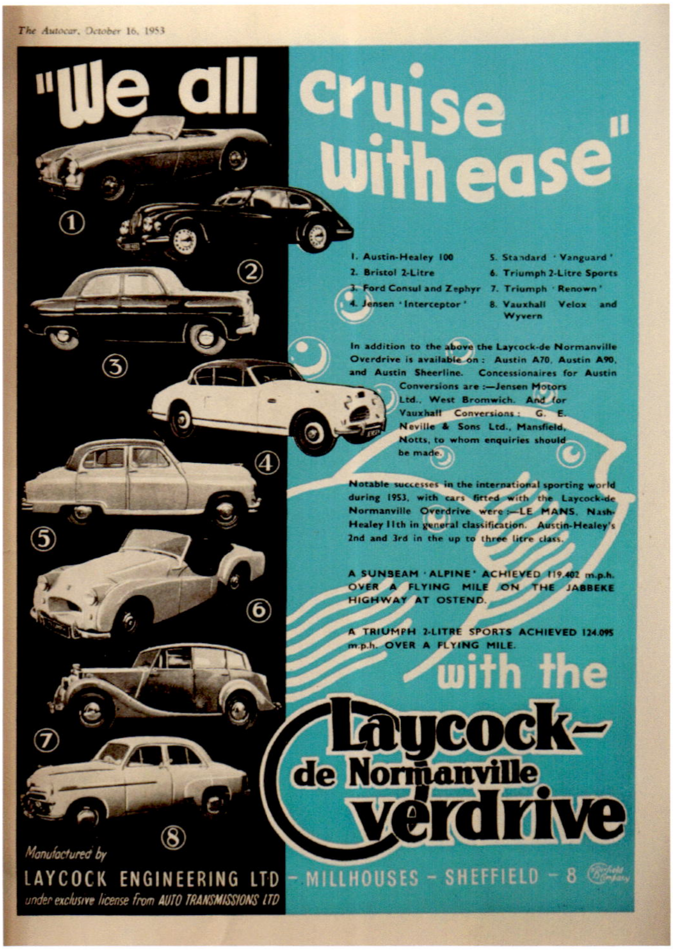

A Laycock de Normanville Overdrive advert.

Model Names and the Naval Connection

The Mayflower model name was clearly chosen to exploit the historic links of the ship with the American market. Later Herald and Standard variants such as Pennant and Ensign appeared, therefore the Renown name was clearly an early example of a marine or naval connection, along with the Vanguard.

There were at least two British warships named HMS *Renown*, but, more interestingly, my good friend Tom Robinson was probably the first to identify a direct link with the badge of the battleship and the new car's radiator mascot. The mascot can be described as the 'Flaming Torch' version, compared with the somewhat plain, unadorned design preceding it. However, the new mascot must have been influenced by the actual badge of this battleship, described as a 'flaming torch surrounded by laurel leaves'.

It would be easy to assume that the 'Flaming Torch' radiator mascot was introduced right from the start of Renown production. In fact, only those cars made after TDB 3001 in 1950 were originally fitted with the improved mascot, though many earlier versions have been retrofitted with the new version. While the 'torch symbol' played no part in Triumph history again, the 'laurel leaves' were to be used during the 1970s with 'Triumph' in the centre, presumably as a new trademark.

By July 1950, Vanguards were being produced in some numbers: 140 saloons plus thirty vans, but note that no less than 100 CKD (completely knocked down) kits were turned out for export on the same day. In that very same month, though, production of the new

The later radiator mascot – the 'Flaming Torch' design was inspired by the badge of HMS *Renown*. The car had the usual chrome headlamps.

Above: Side view of a typically black TDB Renown.

Left: Colin Pavor of St Sampson, Guernsey, ran this Renown for a time in the early 1960s.

Mayflower started on 3 July, though prototypes had been assembled in late 1949. It is estimated that just over 2,900 TDB Renowns were built in 1950.

The model continued into 1951 and on one random spring day SMC records showed an output of no less than 320 cars, including twenty Renowns. This was easily eclipsed as usual by Vanguard production and now also by Mayflowers, with sixty units made, including twenty CKD kits for assembly abroad.

Production had been slow to ramp up initially, but in late 1951 production of this traditional-looking car was clearly selling in reasonable numbers for a 'halo model' in the Standard-Triumph line-up of the time. From TDB 5966 (in 1951), headlamp shells and rims were body painted instead of chrome, a move that was reversed when chrome and nickel supplies were available again in 1952 (from TDC 1619), but this is jumping ahead of the story. This is believed to be all a direct result of the Korean War, but most cars had chrome headlamp shells.

Meanwhile, the Vanguard Phase I had been updated in 1952 to a revised Phase IA format, with changes limited to a new bolder grille and a larger rear window. By now, however, a replacement was being considered: the Phase II – in my opinion a rather unhappy notchback design introduced in 1953, which seemed to somehow emphasise even more its short overall length and consequently truncated appearance.

It is known that 6,500 complete TDB cars were produced, plus TDB 6501, which in chassis form was passed to the Experimental Department according to SMC records. In a UK-wide search for these cars in the remaining licensing records, my colleague Tom Robinson found that it had subsequently acquired a body, registered as EDN 520, and it was built on 19 December 1951. However, a few pilot-production TDC Renowns with the longer wheelbase were also built tin the latter part of 1951, as will be discussed shortly.

There was to be no other significant changes to the first series Renown during its run. The annual production totals were:

Year	Production	Commission Number
1949	92	(TDB 1–92)
1950	3,148	(TDB 93–3240)
1951	3,261	(TDB 3241–6501)
Total number of units built: 6,501		

7

The Long Wheelbase Renown – TDC Prefix

Perhaps surprisingly at this stage, the model life of the Renown was extended in late 1951 with the aim of making a longer wheelbase Limousine version, with Commission Numbers preceded by TDC vs TDB of the earlier version. The aim was to allow more comfort for rear-seat passengers.

The main change was that the 108-inch wheelbase, which applied to all previous versions, was now increased to 111 inches. The extra 3 inches were hardly noticeable from a side view and were concentrated entirely in the cabin area, divided roughly two-thirds/ one-third in favour of rear-seat passengers.

Some people refer to this longer wheelbase version being the Mk II, though this was never used by the makers, nor can I find any mention of it in any contemporary articles. Similarly, Triumph literature does not use the terms 'Series Two' or 'long-wheelbase' to describe the new version of the Renown.

On 27 August 1951, the prototype saloon (Cotman Grey with grey interior) was constructed, with first Limousine following on 31 August 1951 as TDC 2001-LIM on 31 August 1951. This car was Jade Green with brown upholstery, consistent with the showroom folder now available which featured both the new saloon and the introduction of the Limousine.

TDC 1 was probably built in November or December 1951, with TDC 2 built on 19 December 1951 when the last TDB was also going down the line. Apart from different doors and handles, the easiest way to recognise the TDC Renown is the larger back window with the new air vent on the scuttle. Otherwise, the car was very similar looking to the TDB, especially from the three-quarter front aspect of the traditional photograph.

With the alternative option making two different chassis, it had made commercial sense to rationalise; therefore, the TDC Renown saloon now benefited from the longer wheelbase of the Limousine. With the new model launch you might have expected an advertising campaign along the lines of 'new, improved 'Renown, with longer wheelbase, more internal room etc'. However, this did not happen and nothing seemed to be made of these significant advantages in advertising material, so the change was made with no fanfare, consistent with the original launch of the TDB Renown.

The front end of a 1953 TDC Renown.

It seemed to me logical to deal with the 'ordinary' saloon model first, since the Commission Numbers involved were both the first and last to be made, with the Limousines mainly in one single block of numbers.

Surprisingly, there was no prestigious catalogue to help sell either car and give it a sense of exclusivity and luxury, though the artwork was a considerable improvement on the literature that had preceded it. Whether you wanted to order a saloon or a Limousine, you got the same relatively cheap-to-produce, but at least colourful, folder of the type given to schoolchildren at showrooms and motor shows!

In December 1951, the most expensive Vanguard was the estate, complete with radio and heater, costing £1,029 14*s.* 5*d.* (£1,294.72) inclusive of purchase tax. Compared with that somewhat utilitarian vehicle, the Renown was surely good value at £825 plus tax, or a showroom price of £1,294 16*s.* 8*d.* (£1,294.84). The Limousine was priced at £895 or £1,383 14*s.* 5*d.* (£1,383.72) tax inclusive, plus optional Overdrive at £54 8*s.* 11*s.* (£54.45). By contrast, the Mayflower was available at £654 16*s.* 8*d.* (£654.85) including tax but with vynide trim. Or you could purchase a better-equipped car for £731 16*s.* 8*d.* (£731.85), but at least this would get you leather trim plus a radio and heater (again, tax inclusive).

The adverts for the TDC version in the motoring press and upmarket magazines were very odd, too. Many showed a very dominant colour photo of a typically British scene (such as a village cricket match in progress) with the strapline 'All that's best in Britain' and a tiny

Above: Filming an episode of the popular TV programme *Bangers and Cash*, now in its tenth series, featuring the late Chris Hewitt's TDC Renown.

Below: A portrait of the late Chris Hewitt's 1953 TDC Renown (LOR 664).

side view of a Renown underneath. Was it supposed to be a tourist-related advert aimed at enticing people to visit this country from abroad or designed to sell cars, I wonder? Even the showroom publicity material for the humbler Mayflower and Standard Eight models generally had more attractive artwork than that for these top-of-the-range SMC models.

Two separate blocks of Commission Numbers were allocated to saloons, with 189 numbers originally reserved for Limousines within the saloon production series of numbers. Please read on to find out in the next chapter about further orders not revealed in the official statistics.

Thanks to the generosity of the late David Blackwell, long associated with the Standard Motor Club (and once a Flying Standard V8 owner too), I borrowed a batch of the surviving copies of the 1954 SMC production records to comb through. These tomes filled a substantial suitcase but only covered about six months! In carrying out this exercise, I could identify the final batch of Renowns, which had previously been available in just five standard colours as mentioned earlier, but I now found some surprising special orders (such as two-tone) never before offered. It seems you could have any colour you liked at this stage in the production run.

By May 1952, you could buy a Renown saloon or Limousine for £925 (excluding tax), compared with the Rover P4 75 at £955 or, say, a Lanchester Fourteen at £985 or, in a slightly lower bracket, a Riley 1.5 litre at £860. No Jaguar was available under £1,000 and the cheapest Bentley Standard Saloon was £3,100; all figures exclude tax. It is difficult to explain, though, how the Limousine was now available at the very same price so soon after its introduction, unless it was simply not selling.

Production Numbers

In 1952, daily production was down to mere single figures on many days, even with the improved rear legroom and a (low-key) relaunched car. However, on 20 August 1952, a more impressive total of no less than ten Renowns were made out of 140 cars in all, a day perhaps more notable for intriguingly recording that fifteen CKD Vanguard kits were exported to Imperia in Belgium to be converted to LHD convertible format. Only one convertible Vanguard is believed to have survived from an earlier batch, and this example has since been converted to RHD.

Only 1,400 TDC Renowns were completed in 1952 versus 12,000 Mayflowers, and that car too was struggling in the marketplace.

The year 1953 was notable for seeing the first Phase II Vanguard completed on New Year's Day (not a public holiday until many years later). That June the first new small Standard to be produced since the end of Flying Standard production, the budget model Standard Eight, was oddly recorded in the production records as a 'Standard Eight Mayflower'. (While it is really beyond the scope of this book, the later upmarket Standard Pennant model, which came later, was originally going to be badged as a 'new' Triumph Mayflower, with one mocked-up example produced; however, export versions intended for the USA were rebadged as a Triumph Ten in sedan and estate wagon format – Standards not being sold stateside.)

With the model fast attaining 'run-out' status, production had dropped to a trickle by 1953. By early 1953, it was reported that no fewer than 431 Renowns were still in stock and

Above: A TDC Renown on the Isle of Wight in September 2024 (MAR 521).

Left: A mock-up for a possible new Triumph Mayflower based on the Standard Ten – the 1957 Pennant model could have been developed from this concept. (Courtesy of BMIHT, Gaydon)

production was down to only two per day vs fourteen units daily three years earlier. At this stage, another 965 Renowns were expected to be built to complete the run, including two Limousines. In fact, six more of the latter were to be built after the main 1951/52 production run.

But despite all the hype for the Mayflower, the Renown was still being produced after Mayflower production had stopped in 1953, with about 34,000 units built. However, the last batch of Mayflowers delivered to the USA were said to have been raffled to avoid the cost of sending them back here as they were unable to be sold. Perhaps that is why some were resprayed in yellow.

Not surprisingly, the end of production of the TDC Renown was considered, but apparently this would have meant a cancellation charge to Mulliners of Birmingham, who made the coach-built bodies. Therefore, in all probability the model continued beyond its natural lifespan. Ominously, though, by mid-1953 there were still 341 Renowns in factory stock, which by February 1954 was down to a still far from respectable 246 and cancellation was again mooted.

The End of Production in 1954

In July 1954, *The Autocar* reported that the Renown had its price reduced substantially to £1,136 11s. 8*d*. (£1,136.59) including tax. As a comparison, in May 1953 saloons and Limousines were still at the very same price of £1,440 7*s*. (£1,440.35) including tax but excluding optional Overdrive at an unchanged extra cost.

Naturally, the car altered very little in this final period of production. Sadly, the last Renown TDC 2799 was built on 28 October 1954, with production quietly phased out. TDC 2800 was also scheduled to be built on the very same day, as the records show, but the sanction was subsequently cancelled. By this time the car was still elegant in the eyes of many, but realistically it could not compete with the likes of contemporaries such as the gradually improving Rover P4 series, Riley Pathfinder, Ford Zephyr and Zodiac, plus the Jaguar Mk VII, Humber Hawk and so on, all with more modern styling.

Many Renowns were to linger on in dealer showrooms into 1955 because the car was still listed as a 'current model', but this was common practice to assist the dealer network to dispose of the final unsold examples. Its somewhat antiquated appearance at this stage draws comparison with the famous 'Auntie Rover P4' almost ten years later, when that car lingered on in production into summer 1964 after fifteen years as a current model but with numerous mechanical and body improvements along the way. The big difference here, though, is that by 1964 there were the P5 and P6 models in the range (the 3-litre and smaller 2000 models respectively), whereas the only other Triumph available in 1954 was the very different TR2 sports car.

Therefore, this was the end of the Triumph Razoredge saloon. Mayflower production had already ceased by 1953, leaving the Renown as the last Triumph saloon of any type to be made until the advent of the smaller, Michelotti-designed 'Herald' in 1959 – that is, providing you exclude the export-only and badge-engineered Triumph Ten, based on a Standard Ten.

8

Renown Limousine – TDC Prefix with the Suffix LIM

Apart from the internal differences, the production Limousine was outwardly identical to the standard TDC Renown. However, the first Limousine carried a fuel filler flap not unlike that on the Roadster. Naturally, a division was included, but the radio was still optional and other internal comforts for 'sir' and 'madam' such as ducted heating were standard fitments. Meanwhile, the poor chauffeur had to put up with a less luxurious and uncomfortable-looking non-adjustable seat. Though, in fairness, when I had the chance of driving a superb example in Texas in 2016 at the Vintage Triumph Register Convention it was not as uncomfortable as I had expected, and I say this as I have a 6-foot frame. This was all thanks to the courtesy – and bravery — of owner Dave Pilcher (who is even taller than I am!). It was the very same car, and first example of a Limousine, I had ever seen in 1976 at the first TROC Rally.

I have been unable to find any detail on how the Limousine concept came about. Some key SMC figures went as far as to deny that any longer wheelbase car had ever been made –

Not all Limousines look immaculate; this one had terminal rear-end rot. It was to be converted into an estate car (see p. 86).

A Renown Limousine pictured at a rally in Britain, Coventry-registered LVC 313. It was later exported to the USA.

and this was back in the mid-1970s when only around twenty years had elapsed since the model was in production.

Nevertheless, there was clearly still some demand for a classically designed car of this type in Britain, and parts of the Commonwealth too. Therefore, production continued with the Limousine version yielding potential new customers for whom a Rolls-Royce or Bentley would perhaps be too ostentatious and much more expensive at about four times the price.

Another rival model to the Triumph Limousine was provided by Austin, which produced the razor-edge A125 Sheerline model from 1947 to compete with Rolls-Royce and Bentley. This model was also made in both standard wheelbase form, and from 1949 as a limousine. The latter had an 11-foot wheelbase (just over a foot longer than the regular saloon) and a much larger 3,995cc power plant adapted from the Austin Lorry.

By contrast, an Austin Sheerline Limousine cost £1,599 plus tax and the top-of-the range A135 Princess Saloon equivalent was even dearer at £1,903, so it can be seen that the Triumph version was in a price class of its own at just £925 plus tax. (All these prices were correct in May 1952.) However, it was a smaller car with just a four-cylinder 2,088cc engine, but it did look the part in my view.

The first batch of Renown Limousines would appear to run from 2001 LIM to 2189 LIM, but when an order came in late in the day for the 190 Limousine for British Railways, 2190 had already been allocated for the TDC Saloon series. As such, it was decided to allocate the number TDC 3000 LIM, which would allow plenty of room for the rest of the saloon

Above and below: The same car owned by Dave Pilcher in Texas, which I was allowed to drive at a Vintage Triumph Register Convention in 2016.

A portrait of an immaculate Triumph Mayflower, Coventry-registered LKV 558.

production to be numbered in sequence. It was clearly expected at the time to be the last of its type. How strange then that this highest number Renown was not the last built.

Extended Production Life

Most production Renown Limousines were built during 1952, just after it had been officially launched. An order for three Limousines was fulfilled during 1953, however, with another batch of three to follow in 1954. It is not known how these two later orders came to be ordered and built, but because there were no spare numbers within those already earmarked these additional six had various numbers allocated within the saloon series, though the numbers for the final three 1954 production were consecutive. Those final three are believed to have come from an American order, as two of the three have been traced to the USA many years later, including the very last to be made – TDC 2622 LIM.

Traditionally built, but modernised over the years both mechanically and within the cabin, I wonder if there was any other saloon car being produced in reasonable numbers anywhere in the world in this time-honoured form like the Renown? Traditional, hand-built sports cars like Morgans have long had some of these features and still incorporate certain aspects to this day, as do subsequent retro models introduced much more recently too (like the Panther), but these were hand-built specialist sports cars, constructed in relatively small numbers. After all, the Renown was still being built as late as 1954 with a traditional ash-framed coach-built body on a separate chassis, and still with separate wings and running boards, separate head and side lamps, an upright radiator grille and externally mounted radiator cap. This was in direct contrast to the then almost universal envelope style for saloon cars and indeed many sports cars, not least its stablemate TR2, mainly introduced post-war.

9

The Mayflower – The Small Razoredge Car

Significant hopes were attached to the Mayflower, introduced ahead of the plain Standard Eight and Ten models to come in 1953/54. Once again, the large Razoredge cars were to be upstaged by the junior models when it came to the publicity drive, which for the Mayflower had started in March 1949 – well ahead of the launch at the autumn 1949 motor show.

A specially produced enlarged weekly issue of *The Autocar* from mid-April 1950 majored on the new model and a whole variety of brochures were issued to cover overseas territories such as Australia, Portugal, South Africa, Sweden and even Japan, plus North America, as well as the home market. Most of those were very much more colourful than those produced for its larger brother, though they were only folders rather than the more prestigious catalogues or booklets produced for the senior models.

A pair of Triumph Mayflowers (note the differing treatment of the rear windows), with the earlier model on the left.

A column gear change featured with a relatively large and airy cabin, much like the Renown in concept, but it is fair to say that it was not overpowered with its 1,247cc engine.

The Mayflower was SMC's first unitary construction car – a notable first in the firm's history. There was even a 'ghost version' of the car displayed at the 1949 motor show, constructed in such a way as to reveal its mechanical parts. This one-off model did not last long enough to be preserved, but I am told it did survive for at least a couple of decades in a school in the Midlands.

It followed a one-model policy strongly encouraged by the then Labour government – the Vanguard was one of the best examples of this policy at work in the British motor industry. The model had replaced all the previously available post-war Flying Standards until the new budget Standard Eight and Ten models were introduced. Therefore, with just two large (by British standards) saloon cars and the Roadster in production in early 1949, including the new Vanguard, there was clearly a major gap to be filled for a smaller car in the range, with greater sales potential especially in the home country, just as predicted back in that original 1946 press release.

The American Market

In the USA, after the war, four-cylinder cars were virtually unknown; a 'small car' over there would 'only' have a six cylinder of about 3 litres (or more). Even that would often be regarded as a compromise purchase when compared with an eight-cylinder version of much the same looking car, coupled with a reduction in external trim and a less luxurious interior to justify a lower price.

Despite this background, the Mayflower was conceived as light car challenger for the American market, trading on its evident link of model name with the country's very

A Mayflower is contrasted with David Shulver's 1800 Saloon.

origins. Its 'Britishness' could perhaps also have been a selling point, while its unique appearance was quite unlike anything else on the road over there (or indeed over here) and thus would be easily recognisable.

After all, only a decade or so later the Volkswagen Beetle came along which was also a small four-cylinder car. It was often bought as a second car with no obvious appeal on paper and it, too, looked unlike any other car on the road, and yet was hugely successful. Unlike the Mayflower, the Beetle was not even originally designed with USA exports in mind; moreover, it also had the major disadvantage of a very unhappy historical link, and this relatively soon after the Second World War.

Pricing Problems and the Competition

A major barrier was to be price. A letter from an American reader writing in a British motoring magazine in May 1947 explained the position eloquently:

> I would very much like to own a Bentley, Triumph Roadster [various other British makes were listed] and appreciate real perfection in design and workmanship, but your prices are out of reach, even neglecting [*sic*] freight and import expenses.
>
> The cheapest of these costs more than a Cadillac or Packard Super Eight in this country.

Both the American cars were, of course, examples of luxury marques with eight-cylinder engines, and this was at a time when £1 bought US $2.56. (At the time of writing £1 = US $1.24, though it has headed towards parity very recently before recovering.)

The Mayflower did take Razoredge styling in a very different direction, but it was not coach-built like the Renown. Yet, from the rear, it looked very like its larger brother.

It is known that the body was designed by Leslie Moore, Chief Body Designer of Mulliners, Birmingham, who later headed up design at Standard-Triumph after the former firm was absorbed by SMC. The bodyshells were built by Fisher & Ludlow at Castle

Triumph Mayflower grille – a bird's-eye view.

Bromwich, Birmingham, now the home of Jaguar cars. Spitfires were also once built here – the planes, I mean! Waler Belgrove did not think much of this car either and said so many years later, so it is clear that he had nothing to do with this design.

The radiator grille looked very like a modified Renown grille but with a slimmer profile; the bumpers were of the same section and it had the very same overriders as those of the Renown too. I know this as two brand-new overriders were unbolted from a still-protected, as shipped, front bumper blade in my presence at Greenwich Autos, south-east London, then later refitted to my own Renown. Perhaps I should now apologise to the unlucky purchaser of that Mayflower bumper, though that was back in around 1971!

The Oldest Surviving Mayflower Turns Up in 2016 – X488

I have mentioned that the model was launched at the 1949 British Motor Show with great fanfare. It is known that a number of prototypes were built and, remarkably, one of these survives to this day in the USA. This car is X488 with original Coventry registration number JWK 612.

This very car was featured in road tests in two top-selling British car magazines of the time (*The Autocar* and *The Motor*), on the cover of at least one sales brochure and was even the subject of extensive testing within Europe, culminating in the production of a dedicated publicity brochure – *5000 Miles in Europe*.

After purchase from SMC it was taken by its proud second owner, Cyril Cockerill, hailing from Hull, to Canada. It also travelled many miles in the USA after its owner moved south of the border. It is surely the most travelled Mayflower in the world, including the time when it was being used by its makers.

It was saved from the scrapman at the very last moment by Kyia Friesen, a motor spares specialist, and is currently awaiting restoration. It was bought by Dennis Delargy, whose nephew, Jason Dennis, tells the story:

> Kyia seen X488 for sale on Craigslist.com and it piqued his interest. He bought it from a man who runs a scrapyard in California who bought the car from Cyril Cockerill's widow in Lancaster, California, Mohave Desert area.
>
> I believe Kyia drove quite a distance to view the car but decided it was too much of a project and initially declined to buy it ... then while sitting in a cinema waiting for the movie to start, he was browsing eBay and stumbled across the '5000 miles through Europe in a Triumph Mayflower' booklet for sale and recognised the Registration number – JWK 612 – from the photos in the 1950 brochure.
>
> Knowing this he bought the car and started researching online the Chassis Number X488. He wrote to *The Automobile Magazine* and the late Michael Worthington-Williams OBE (1938–2021) posted the discovery in his 'Finds and Discoveries' column which confirmed it was the 4th Prototype Mayflower made by Triumph and then Kyia later advertised it himself for sale.
>
> I believe that Cyril Cockerill's widow sold X488 for scrap value after her husband passed away ... He owned X488 in Hull, UK then imported the car to Canada Iin 1962 and he still kept it while moving from job to job, first New York then Los Angeles area before settling in Lancaster, California, in the Mohave Desert area.

Prototype Mayflower X488 JWK 612, discovered in California and saved from scrap by Kyia Friesen. (Courtesy of Kyia Friesen)

Even now, I can clearly recall that the small car did seem to capture the imagination of the general public, certainly from a recognition viewpoint. Perhaps this was because of its unique and quirky styling. It was sadly not a success as far as sales were concerned, especially in North America, the market that was its specific target.

Variations on the Mayflower Theme

John Davy in his 1967 Standard history book also revealed the existence of a Mayflower 'Ute' conversion, or pick-up truck, built up from CKD kits in Port Melbourne in Victoria, Australia. In addition, a small number of convertible Mayflowers were built, modified from standard saloons by Mulliners of Birmingham, none of which are believed to survive, though a much later conversion was often to be seen on the rally field in the 1990s.

The story of this model might be summed up in a sad 1953 panoramic photo I have seen. It shows an untold number of completed new cars looking for buyers stored in a quarry in an area in Baginton to the south-east of Coventry, which is now occupied by Coventry Airport.

Only 510 examples were exported to the USA during production, whereas perhaps not even 100 of its larger stablemate reached those shores. For those that remain, however, there is an enthusiastic following, though personally I have yet to see a Mayflower in North America. However, in Britain the smaller Razoredge Triumphs always attract attention from the general public and are frequently to be seen at TROC and other rallies. They make a charming contrast with Roadsters, the larger Saloons and the occasional alternative Phase I or II Vanguard.

Above: Only in Australia: a Mayflower Ute. (TROC Archives)

Below: The Mayflower convertible. It is a modern conversion because no original Mulliner conversions are believed to have survived.

10

After the Renown

No car really succeeded the Renown until the Triumph 2000 Saloons of 1963 to 1977, produced in two 'marks', but that does not mean to say that there was no consideration given at the time, as I will discuss below.

A Possible Replacement from 1949 – and Another from an Unknown Date

It is known that as early as 1949 Mulliner was working on a possible replacement design that would follow more modern practice. It would still have an upright radiator grille, but have a more integrated Razoredge body design, complete with built-in lights and wings. The model was vaguely reminiscent of the later Armstrong-Siddeley Sapphire and tried to marry a traditional upright radiator into a modern envelope-style body with suggested front and rear wings. The superb scale model had an opening boot and miniature luggage, as illustrated earlier in this book. Chris Moore, the son of the late Les Moore (of Mulliners and Triumph), told me that Les made and designed that model in that very year, but the concept was not pursued. Incidentally, that 1949 model was sold at an auction in 2019, but incorrectly attributed to the late Stuart Peck. However, this mention of Les does give me the opportunity to draw attention to the last model of a Renown he made shortly before he died, and I believe the photo speaks for itself.

There were other full-sized mock-ups built later (date unknown) by SMC, which were not attractive to say the least. They had the same body with various hideous radiator grilles, some harking back to pre-war cars from various other makers.

The Vanguard-based Renown that Became the Sportsman Just Before Launch

It was thanks to the 1967 John Davy book on SMC (mentioned earlier) that I first found out about the stillborn Renown version of the then new Vanguard Phase III. This was

A 1956 Standard Sportsman, which was going to be the successor to the TDC Renown but there was a very late change of heart.

introduced at the 1955 London Motor Show, followed by an estate version the following year.

While it might not look so now, in its day the Phase III was a much more balanced and successful design, with its somewhat scaled-down American styling. Remember, the original Phase I Vanguard was inspired by the 1942 Plymouth, but, constrained by its wheelbase, was really too short to be a harmonious design. However, now with the obvious lack of a 'halo' model, the possibility of a badge-engineered upmarket Triumph version of this car was seriously considered, but eventually produced as the 'Standard Sportsman'.

The Commission Numbers were placed in the Triumph series with a TDD prefix logically following on from the final TDC Renowns. Personally, I liked that modernised version of that Renown radiator grille, with a Triumph 'Globe' placed centrally placed at the top and on the steering wheel boss. Photographs were taken before launch, but to my knowledge these have never been published until now. They show the car with Renown badges in script on the front wing and boot, but I do not believe any made it to showrooms for sale in this form.

Examples of Sportsman cars are now very rare indeed and it was many years before I saw one, even when new. They were very distinctive and usually found in two-tone bright colours, though one well-known example is finished in monotone green, but there is no mistaking the car with that Triumph-style grille.

At this time Walter Belgrove left SMC in a huff at the 1955 London Motor Show where the Phase III made its debut; he never worked in the motor industry again.

By now, with the Mayflower gone, Triumph was only building a single model: the TR2, a somewhat incongruous stablemate for the Renown when that model was in production. Consequently, there was to be no saloon model to bear the Triumph name until the Herald came out at the end of the 1950s, unless you count that previously mentioned Triumph Ten, the badge-engineered Standard Ten for the USA market.

Left: This modern take on a Triumph radiator grille adorns a production Standard Sportsman.

Below: This is a very early version of the same car but badged as a Triumph Renown. (Courtesy BMIHT, Gaydon)

A Standard Sportsman unusually produced in monotone green – most cars were two-tone.

This new model, as its model name implies, clearly had sporting pretensions and might have been regarded as a precursor of the 1960s Triumph Vitesse and Dolomite Sprint from the 1970s. On this basis alone it was a strange choice to follow the traditional Renown, and no doubt second thoughts prevailed. Therefore, the Phase III Standard Sportsman was launched instead in 1955.

The Phase III's rear lights were very much like those on American Fords, but overall the car was distinctive in its own way. The main innovation for this Standard model was its unitary construction, following the lead of the earlier Mayflower, then the Eight and Ten models. The grille resembled a 1954 Plymouth (that marque cropping up once again in the story) with its oval opening bisected by a prominent horizontal steel moulding.

Indeed, the Renown replacement which eventually came into production had itself a short life initially, as will be seen, and was a totally different car from those potential replacements mentioned earlier. Garish colour schemes applied to the Sportsman model were not exactly in the Triumph tradition, but bore further evidence of transatlantic influence.

The Sportsman had different bumpers, overriders and other features to distinguish the car from the lesser Standard models. However, at £1,231 on announcement in August 1956 the car was too expensive in its class to be competitive. It must have had a fair turn of speed, though, with its twin-carburettor 2,138cc engine with Overdrive – a sort of early GT model. Commission Numbers ran from TDD 1–901 for the saloon version and TDD 902–5 for the estate version, for the initial batch of vehicles, but please see below.

When the estate car version of the Phase III model came out a Sportsman Estate was also produced, which could have been a Renown Estate if things had worked out differently. It is known that five were made in right-hand-drive form and exported to Canada.

Oddly enough, while it was a Sportsman mechanically speaking, it is understood to have lacked the external distinctive Triumph styling features such as the radiator grille.

For a long time it was understood that the Sportsman version was only made from 1955 until 1957, which makes sense when it was hardly selling that well, as has been demonstrated. That should surely have been the end of the story, but as with the extended life of the Renown Limousine the model quietly lived on without being 'listed', with at least these additional cars made after the reported end of production:

- 1959: Twenty Sportsman Saloons and nineteen more estate cars are manufactured, with two and six exported respectively.
- 1960: The numbers made are now reduced to just eight saloons and nine estates, with just one estate exported.

Note that no less than thirty-three estate versions were made in all. As with many other production statistics set out earlier, all these details have emerged from Phil Homer's diligent and no doubt time-consuming research reproduced in *Triumph World* articles.

Incidentally, the chosen name of 'Sportsman' was a very odd choice because it had been used by both Ford and Chrysler in the USA before, and, closer to home, Daimler also produced their own very different Sportsman model in 1956. This model had a coach-built body designed and made by Mulliners of Birmingham. One wonders how two major British car makers could come up with the same model name at the same time without apparently any legal wrangling – those were very different times!

Thus, the Razoredge story ends with a Mulliners of Birmingham connection and a last-minute changed model name, too – very appropriately, of course, and just as it started.

11

Close Relations and Celebrations

I wanted to include this chapter to cover the miscellaneous one-offs, interesting conversions and vehicles that did not fit into the previous chapters. I will deal with them in the order in which I discovered them.

This beautiful wooden model was completed by ex-Mulliners and SMC Design Chief Les Moore after his retirement.

Above: Massey Ferguson Works Emergency Force – underneath that Vanguard Ambulance is a Renown TDC chassis.

Below: I saw this pick-up truck conversion by chance in Atherton, Lancashire, but I was too shocked to snap it at the time. Luckily a photo came from another source. (TROC Archives)

Above: I tracked this one down in Coventry and it came to one of the rallies. Owner Bill Moore used it regularly at the time for his business.

Below: Tom Dolby owns this rare Ambulance, seen here in 2013. It is one of only three made and possibly the sole survivor.

Above: The distressed Limousine pictured was being converted by the late Chris Hewitt to an estate car – the only Limo estate car in the world?

Left: Finally, Mulliners gets a well-deserved credit on the bulkhead under the bonnet of Tom's Ambulance.

Below: Tom Dolby also owns this Renown breakdown truck. The famous (and much mocked) Milton Keynes concrete cows admire the vehicle in silence at the TROC Rally, 2023.

Above left: A Meccano model, described by them as a 'coupé' but clearly inspired by the Mayflower.

Above right: The same model sits on the bonnet of the real thing.

Below: The three-axle AEC bus is an ex-Leicester Corporation Renown from 1939, which I was lucky enough to travel on to a classic vehicle show in Nottingham. The late local resident Rodney Evans owned the Renown (car) and was persuaded by me to park it alongside the bus for photos, causing some bewildered looks from the bus owners.

TROC's Thirtieth Anniversary in Coventry

In 2005, TROC celebrated its thirtieth anniversary, so a return to Coventry seemed the obvious place to celebrate the marque.

The cars formed up at the Coventry Motor Museum, then headed through the city and into the former Banner Lane shadow factory, latterly the home of tractor makers Massey Ferguson, whose Works Ambulance was featured earlier. The manufacturing area (behind the main office block) had already been razed to the ground, but all the attractive 1930s long office buildings seen in the following photos were demolished just weeks later.

Left: TROC's thirtieth anniversary, or TROC30 for short. No less than six Razoredge cars are seen in Renown Avenue, Coventry, on the site of the Canley factory. Note that the Renown at the front left has the rear window of the TDC model – David Wickens' immaculate HRY 79.

Below: TROC30. Coventry Motor Museum is the start of the rally.

The offices had been in a 1960s office tower in an area nearest the road, but when I went back it was an empty site with only the gates and perimeter wall remining. On the same day we felt we had to go to Renown Avenue, on the old Fletchamstead Highway SMC site in Canley where adjacent roads also take former SMC model names. Some cars parked for a short time outside the nearby Standard-Triumph Sports & Social Club too.

Above and below: TROC30. The cars line up outside the attractive 1930s Banner Lane offices just weeks before the demolition squad moved in. (Courtesy of Mike Sampson)

Reproducing the original locations used for the PR photo shoot undertaken in 1950 forty-three years later. This is the former home of Lord Kenilworth in Leamington, who was born John Siddeley.

The event culminated in a gathering at Coombe Abbey Park to the very east of the city. Needless to say it was the most ambitious event ever planned, but there was no time to visit the SMC Service Depot with its attractive art deco features, found on the north side of the A45 to the west of the city.

In 1993, I decided to try to track down the principal scenic locations used for publicity shots in Warwickshire and the Cotswolds, all chosen when the Renown was brand new. The images that follow are the result.

More recently, I spotted an image in a 1950s motoring magazine.

Then, as a tribute to the range of talents within SMC's principal sub-contractor, Mulliners of Birmngham, how about this futuristic (for the 1950s) coach designed and built on a Guy chassis and famously modelled by Tri-ang in their Spot On range?

And then, to finish off this section of the book, this pre-war MG Saloon radiator grille seems so close to the Triumph's (apart from the badge and mount) that I wonder if SMC saved costs by requesting relatively minor changes to the tooling to produce a handsome grille for the then new 1800 Saloon and all later models?

Above, below and overleaf above: Claverdon Forge. Nigel and Sue Orrett's Renown substitutes for the original SMC Fleet car. It was still operating as a forge then but by August 2024 was a shop. It has recently been put up for sale and will need a new tenant.

Below: Since being partially destroyed by fire, this formerly attractive half-timbered inn at Preston Bagot, near Henley-in-Arden, had an uncertain future when I saw it in August 2024.

Above: A commonly reproduced photo in its original form. The Broadway Hotel was also used as a backdrop by the Rootes official snapper for shooting the then new Minx.

Below: Freestone & Webb had nothing to do with Triumph car designs but note the text in this 1952 advert.

This futuristic Guy Warrior coach was designed and bodied by Mulliner of Birmingham. Did Les Moore design it, I wonder?

Above left: This pre-war radiator grille is fitted to an MG saloon car but looks suspiciously like that of the Razoredge models, apart from the badge and mount.

Above right: Triumph's version of the grille.

Afterword

What to Look for When Buying a Razoredge Car

When these cars were being made, I imagine that the expected lifespan was little more than twenty to twenty-five years at the most. Little thought was given to rustproofing at the time, making corrosion the biggest potential problem some seventy years later, plus (unlike modern cars) deterioration of the ash frame. Check under the front wings to see if the coach bolts connecting the wings to the body still pass through the ash frame and that there is not just 'fresh air'.

The front chassis cross-member corroded badly within just over twenty years of service in the case of both Renowns I owned, not helped by my living near the coast with its salty air.

The front floorboards are wooden, so easily replaced, but the rear steel cabin floor corroded badly during my five-year ownership. Other problem areas are found on the steel bodywork including around the rear wings and the guttering above the side windows.

Thanks to aluminium doors, bonnet lids, boot lid, etc., fitted throughout production, these items are less of a problem if the ash framing is still intact. Steering is very heavy and takes its toll on both the driver and the steering components, including kingpins and track-rod ends, with regular greasing being essential to prevent undue wear.

There are some definite plus points when considering purchase if the following improvements have already been made: Overdrive gearbox, an electric fan in front of the radiator (to deal with today's traffic conditions) and, most essential in my view, the fitment of servo-assisted brakes for precisely the same reason.

The author would be very pleased to receive any contemporary (non-factory) photos of the 1800 and 2000 Saloon and Renown models featured in this book, and indeed any personal stories or recollections of the cars.

Please write to the author via the Amberley Publishing or email me at johnbath@hotmail.co.uk.

As there are probably more car clubs for the Triumph marque than any other car make, for further information on the classic car clubs mentioned head to websites for the following:

Triumph Razoredge Owners Club Ltd
Triumph Mayflower Club
Triumph Roadster Club
Standard Motor Club

There is only one car club that caters for pre-war models made by the original Triumph Car Company: Pre-1940 Triumph Motor Club.

Thanks for buying, and hopefully enjoying, this book.